Anthony W. Thorold

The Tenderness of Christ

Anthony W. Thorold

The Tenderness of Christ

ISBN/EAN: 9783337022754

Printed in Europe, USA, Canada, Australia, Japan

Cover: Foto ©Lupo / pixelio.de

More available books at **www.hansebooks.com**

THE TENDERNESS OF CHRIST

"*Multitudes are ready to speak for Christ, or to sacrifice themselves in labouring for His cause. But the utterances are too few that come from sitting at His feet, or leaning on His breast.*"

PROFESSOR MILLIGAN.

THE
TENDERNESS OF CHRIST

BY THE LATE RIGHT REV.

ANTHONY W. THOROLD D.D.

LORD BISHOP OF WINCHESTER

Prelate of the Most Noble Order of the Garter
Hon. Fellow of Queen's College Oxford

LONDON
ISBISTER AND COMPANY Limited
15 & 16 TAVISTOCK STREET COVENT GARDEN
1895

> *"If there be good in that I wrought,*
> *Thy hand compelled it master, Thine*
> *Where I have failed to meet Thy thought,*
> *I know through Thee, the blame is mine."*

To

my Dear and only Brother

I Offer this Volume

on a Divine and Ineffable Mystery

the Length and Breadth and Depth and Height

of which we humbly hope to ponder together

in the Life

of the World to Come.

"We have been told that the world has tried the Gospel of Christ and found it wanting. To that the answer is simple: the world has never tried the Gospel of Christ, and in this nineteenth century of the so-called Christian era it has yet to begin."

REV. E. HATCH, D.D.

PREFACE

AN obvious snare, as much for those who attempt to write devotional books as for those who profess to use them, is unreality. There are two sorts of unreality. There is that which fashions ideals and imposes sacrifices, with no sort of purpose either of reaching after the one or consenting to the other. This sort, it may be observed, has at least this merit about it: that it is seen through in a moment. The other, commoner of course, since readers are always more plentiful than writers, is the habit of indulging in a facile emotion about God and heavenly things, which, if not promptly turned into a motive for some devout activity or for the deepening and maturing of personal religion, may soon become the most specious and perilous of all kinds of self-deceit.

It has been said of Bishop Wilson that " he never penned a sentence that savoured of unreality." Who will tell us his secret, or show us how to earn that praise?

The truth of truths is that God is love, and that God in Christ is the expression of it.

> "*In youth I looked to these very skies*
> *And, probing their immensities,*
> *I found God there, His visible power,*
> *Yet felt in my heart amid all its sense*
> *Of the power an equal evidence*
> *That His Love there, too, was the nobler dower."*

Surely Robert Browning would say to us, if we could get an answer from him, that a devotional book, if it is to live and move for an hour, must in a very real sense, though in a figure, be written on the knees. Of course he would bargain that there should be a certain literary quality about it (if it is to be had)—thought, even if brawny and abruptly expressed, some knowledge of human and earthly things incidentally and judiciously interposed, always conduct at the end, and action out of conduct. *Prebendary Eyton.* Unctuousness should be avoided: and "nothing can ever make it safe for us to set ourselves on pinnacles." The one secret to hold fast is manliness. There should be experience, which need not be egoistic because it is fresh and warm with life; for all souls are cast in much the same mould, and, though the lessons of an individual life must not be pressed as evidence, who shall forbid our accepting it as such, if we choose? Beside this, further, there may well be a Divine preparedness for so hallowed a task in that varied, incessant, complete, even awful, life-discipline, which educates as only suffering and the Divine Love can educate, for passing on the lighted torch of the Gospel to the many dark places of human pain. There should also be a profound desire, rooted in the conviction of a very solemn duty, to share with trembling and suffering spirits, who must not lightly be left to tremble and suffer, the fruition of that ineffable and inexhaustible love, which so infinitely transcends in its exquisite and holy tenderness all that lips can utter or thought conceive, which is ever waiting, hoping, offering itself to every human soul that needs it—not easily baffled or wearied, or sent disappointed away.

"A book, like a person, has its fortunes with one; is lucky or unlucky in the precise moment of its falling in our way; and often by some happy incident counts with us for something more than its independent value."

Mr. Pater's agreeable aphorism, translated

into a higher plane of thought and life, encourages the writer to hope that by some such happy accident (and accident is but the result of an unrecognised law) God's good Providence, which is the loftiest region of so-called accident, may occasionally be pleased to bring this humble volume under the notice of any who are honestly seeking after Him, but have not yet found Him as their Father in Christ. Of all happy services, which never can be acknowledged, much less requited, on this side of the grave, but which will assuredly be recognised and requited in the land of old friendships renewed and new friendships born, and where nothing will be forgotten that has brought Christ nearer, or made the Divine will to seem more beautiful and good, among the happiest, often also the most surprising, may be found to be help unconsciously given through an insignificant but sincere book to a troubled soul wandering through twilight hours in some valley of Baca, there to find a well filled with living water, and, perhaps for the first time, to know and believe the love of God.

A. WINTON.

FARNHAM CASTLE,
   Easter, 1891.

CONTENTS

		PAGE
I.	ITS HISTORY	1
II.	ITS PURPOSE	27
III.	ITS METHODS	53
IV.	ITS CLAIMS	81
V.	ITS BLESSEDNESS	105
VI.	ITS RESULTS	129
VII.	IN DEATH	155
VIII.	IN JUDGMENT	183
IX.	IN THE LIFE TO COME	205

"*I long to enjoy Thee in my inmost soul, but I cannot lay hold of Thee.*"

THOMAS À KEMPIS

ITS HISTORY

A

*Take care that you know what Christianity
is before you judge it."*

DEAN CHURCH.

I

ITS HISTORY

" Who loved me and gave Himself for me."
GAL. ii. 20.

LET no one suppose that the Divine mystery, on which I attempt to write now, has only an emotional side to it; or that a subjective way of treating it can adequately exhaust its many practical lessons. While, certainly, no one will care much for it who is altogether a stranger to its blessedness, the subject itself is one of the deepest which the human mind can ponder—so wonderful, so solemn, so elevating that, in spirit, at least, if not in outward reality, we should think of it on our knees. For, as we may see presently, it is the revelation of Eternal God. It is the great secret that underlies the tangled and dark problems of the universe. It is the thought which softens and mellows the griefs and losses of humanity. It is the hope which gilds the horizon of the most clouded life. St. Paul tried to write of it, and failed. But his very failure, while it suggests diffidence, should stir thankfulness. To be able really to believe that we live and move and have our being under the canopy of an infinite tenderness makes this mortal life quite a new thing. For all always to remember that as He has loved us, we also should love one another, would change the face of the world. Of something of the story of this love, as the Gospels describe it, I would write now. To each one severally may God the Holy Ghost graciously and fully impart the teaching he needs. Some are best approached by the way of the understanding.

Rev. J. B. Illingworth. "There are souls, and those among the noblest, to whom the primary avenue of success is the intellect." To others God draws near through the conscience; and by the sense of need, and the burden of sin, offers them light and peace.

Summary. Gal. iv. 4. In what St. Paul calls "the fulness of time"; in what secular historians would describe as that crucial epoch when the Greek philosophy, in all that was vital and sincere, had shifted its centre from Athens to Alexandria; when Roman life, jaded, yet not satiated with wickedness, had settled down into a foul abyss of callous despair; when the imperial civilisation had made journeying easy, intercourse safe, law respected, and trade lucrative; when, not least of all, the Hebrew people, in their isolated strip of territory on the eastern shore of the Midland Sea, fired by the heroism of the Maccabees and stung by the insolence of the Romans, impatiently expected a militant Christ, there dawned upon the world, as at once its surprise, its redemption, and its despair, the humble but unique life of a peasant child. This life, in one sense of the word, was not a long one; in another sense, it was for ever and ever. Chequered by varied incidents, and abruptly terminated by a violent death, by some it has been pronounced a melancholy failure; by others it has been jubilantly welcomed as the regeneration of the world. My one point, at present, is to press on the reader, with as much freshness and earnestness as I can, that the distinguishing quality which, from first to last, permeated, illuminated, hallowed, immortalised it, is love; and that if love is the explanation of its sacrifices, love is also the moral of its duty. "Leaving us an example that ye should follow His steps." Born in an inn stable, and proclaimed to shepherds on the neighbouring hills, from the very first Jesus of Nazareth was educated into sympathy with the toiling millions of mankind. Instantly over His cradle, as afterwards from His own lips, the Gospel was preached to the poor. Twelve years pass, and we have one short glimpse of Him just when the sense of manhood, the thirst for knowledge, the instinct of freedom, the craving for companionship, make the inevitable transition we have all of us experienced when passing from dependent to independent life. For eighteen years more, amid the rough and intolerant peasants of a mountain village, in humble toil, in the favour of men, which could not last, in the favour of His heavenly Father, which could not help lasting, in the bracing discipline of moral and intellectual solitariness, in the dawning hope of a wonderful future, and in the constant fellowship with God over His word, He awaited the summons, which the maturing consciousness of His power, and the solemn mystery of His being, induced Him

1 Pet. ii. 21.

awfully but joyfully to expect. Then, one day Nazareth suddenly missed Him. The call had come; and the place, which had watched His growth, observed His character, admired with a curious envy the gentleness which no one could ruffle, and the purity which nothing could stain, was to know Him no more as it once had known Him in the time of old. In a desert region, on the edge of a melancholy sea, in a mysterious but real conflict with a spiritual adversary, He was tempted like as we are, but without sin. Shortly before, on the banks of a humble river, He had publicly received baptism at a kinsman's hands. Then for the first time, we may reverently believe, the full mystery of His being, the eternal purpose of His birth, the complete plan of His ministry, the unspeakable awfulness of His Passion, were all revealed to Him in a long and inspiring vista, which stirred His joy and nerved His purpose Then, too, He drew to Himself the first of that goodly fellowship of disciples, which has since swelled into a multitude that no man can number, and began to found that Divine kingdom which was to completely win and conquer the world by goodness, and sacrifice, and truth. St. Peter, summarising the public life of his Master, said of Him that "He went about doing good, and healing all that were oppressed of the devil." St. Paul, explaining the reason and the evidence of it, writes, in the words already quoted: "Who loved me, and gave Himself for me."

Acts x. 35.

Gal. ii. 20.

Four groups of facts.

This life may be said to be contained in four groups of facts—His miracles, His teaching, His social relationships, His Passion. We can only touch on them. Each of these chapters in His history—nay, each single incident recorded in them—is but a varying expression, parable, and manifestation of a redeeming and inexhaustible love.

Miracles.

His miracles, which, in one aspect of them, are signs of the kingdom of heaven, and, in another aspect, are instructive instances of an overruling Providence, in yet another are revelations of Divine tenderness. His first was to spare His humble friends the mortification of a meagre hospitality. His last was to requite one who, in the simple discharge of duty—duty aimed against Himself—had severely and perhaps unjustly suffered. When He healed the trembling leper, out of whose crushed soul all self-respect had long ago vanished, He was careful to touch him, as if to say, "I do not despise thy misery, nor loathe thy uncleanness; thou art loved—thou art still a man." When He cured the man blind from his birth, to make the process of healing tangible and reasonable, He made clay of the substance of His own body, anointed him with the clay, and then bade him—by way of giving him his own share in the cure—to wash in Siloam hard by. He did not refuse either to heal or to feed those who simply desired to use His power, though they rejected His friendship. If only they had faith, that was enough for Him. He did what He could do, and He did it for the asking. When He desired to deliver the poor demoniac from the terrible thraldom of the invisible powers of evil, and with the result of sudden destruction to the brute creatures into whose bodies they eagerly entered; it was not that He was indifferent to the sufferings of any part of the sentient creation, which was all the work of His hands, but, as we continually are compelled to observe, because He felt it right to recognise degrees of friendship and kindness suitable for the several ranks of organised being. Clearly it was of more moment that the human captive of Satan should be set instantly and completely free, than that for a few weeks longer the humble creatures, who were ultimately destined to death for the use of men, should prolong an unimportant existence. His way of supplying the material needs of the multitude was rather by removing the causes which, in the shape of disease or sickness, prevented a self-reliant industry, than by encouraging improvidence through constant largesses of food. When He did feed them, it was in the considerateness of a sagacious benevolence, and with a marked and prudent economy of supernatural power. The incessancy, the thoughtfulness, the wisdom, the self-forgetfulness of His acts of healing, all glowed and burned with the fire of love. The blessedness of His public life consisted in the incessant activities of a redeeming and bountiful goodness; and an indescribable humility made it a keen suffering to Him to be praised or admired by the world.

Teaching.   His teaching was given only as men could bear it and could grow into it. It was suited not only to the moral condition, but to the

intellectual capacities of His hearers. Between
the Sermon on the Mount delivered to the
multitude, and the private discourses to His
apostles on the eve of His Passion, there is a
wide gulf, both of precept and doctrine. No
doubt there were occasions, such as the discourse in the synagogue at Capernaum, when
men, His disciples even, were offended, outraged
we might say, by His mysterious and lofty
words. Also, we remember the controversies
both with Sadducees and Pharisees in the last
days of His life, when the dark shadows of the
cross were falling thick and chill on Him, and
when the unfolding of the mystery of His
twofold nature and redeeming purpose could
no longer be suitably concealed. Even at an
earlier time, when the purpose of the religious
leaders had hardened into rejecting Him, He
felt it was only mercy to tell them that no
neutrality was possible in the kingdom of God.
But His rule was to keep back what, in an
immature condition of mind and heart, would
only offend and irritate. He also said, just
before He died, "I have yet many things to *John xvi.
say unto you, but ye cannot bear them now."* 12.
When He privately announced to the apostles

His coming rejection and death, it was with a charge that no man should know it. Full of hope for all who love and try, He was also strong and wise with the patience of hope. He refused to lay on perplexed spirits a greater burden than they then could bear, until at length Pentecost dawned, and the Church was born.

Social relationships. His social relationships were at first simple and few, afterwards became manifold and complicated. His public life soon brought Him into contact with all sorts and conditions of men, and the activities of His ministry drew anxious seekers to His feet. We see Him with His parents, His mother, His brethren. We see Him at a marriage-feast, and we see Him in a Pharisee's house on the Sabbath-day. We see Him the guest of the family of Bethany; we see Him accepting kindness at the hands of Zaccheus. We see Him with His disciples in the borrowed fishing-boats, and on the waters of the stormy sea, when they failed in their faith, and erred in their kindness. The multitude were hungry; and when He had fed them they wanted to make Him a king, but He withdrew Himself. John the Baptist, from his sultry dungeon, sent to ask if He was really the

Christ. Jesus did not answer the question, but gave him evidence by which he might answer it for himself. There could be no respect of persons with Him. A woman came to Him about her demoniac child. First He was silent. When He did speak, His silence was not so troubling as His words. I might easily multiply such occasions, but these are samples, and they may suffice. In each one of them our loving Lord, not with blind rules nor priestly traditions, but by living principles which are for ever, and for us as well as Him, was but as a voice and channel of Divine tenderness. To His parents He showed filial affection, resolute independence, dutiful obedience. He defended Himself, and in defending Himself He expressed a regretful surprise that they had not known Him well enough to make misunderstanding impossible. On His mother, when ignorant as we suppose of the new era of life and duty into which His baptism had introduced Him, unconscious also, as we may think her to have been—the mythical stories of His wonder-working childhood to the contrary—of His supernatural power, she confided to Him the secret of the exhausted resources of the peasant household, in the assurance that, as He had often done before, so He would do again, rescue her from a mortifying embarrassment, He instantly impressed the changed state of things, and that on the activities and methods of His public life she must not claim to intrude. But the way in which He said it must have reassured her. The eye spoke with the lips; and, so far from being chilled or disappointed, in the full assurance of her motherly love, she said to the servants: "Whatsoever He saith unto you, do it." While He showed His love to her in checking an unintentional presumption, He also showed it immediately afterwards by doing far more than she had dared to ask or think, yet so quietly and judiciously that probably hardly a dozen people in the house knew how the supply came. The guests were satisfied, the self-respect of the host protected, the Virgin's heart soothed and contented, and the glory of Jesus not prematurely anticipated by a miracle before their eyes. To His brethren, before they believed on Him, He expressed Himself with quiet dignity, and yet with distinct kindness. The day would come when they would believe on Him. Their faith

John iii. 5.

should wait for its ripeness; He would not hasten it by an hour. But it was better for them, and for Him, that they should go their several ways to the Holy City: "I go not up yet unto the feast; mine hour is not yet come." In Simon's house, where His host did not pay Him the common attention which every guest might claim, the Lord scrupled not, at the risk of wounding his self-love, to contrast the prodigality of the love of the penitent and forgiven sinner with his apparently studied unkindness. At Bethany, when the ever-eager activity of Martha tempted her to resent her sister's inertness, Jesus took the part of her who listened, gently but firmly rebuked the zeal of her who worked. It is not easy to find fault with friends at the moment they are showing us friendliness; only true love can rise to it, love with holiness at its root. From a publican He solicited kindness; for often the shortest and surest way of winning a man is to permit him to serve you. Of the disciples who owed Him everything, He first borrowed a fishing-boat, then magnificently paid for it. When their faith failed His patience seemed to fail—but it was the holy impatience of love. "How long

John vii. 8.

shall I be with you—how long shall I suffer you? Bring him hither to me." The apostle who earned His supreme commendation, also earned His sharp rebuke. The multitude was hungry; and He felt unspeakable pity for them, and fed them. When they came next day for more, all His answer was, "Labour not for the meat which perisheth." It has been accurately and profoundly observed that Jesus never trusted the multitude, though He ever helped them. He did not commit Himself unto them, for He knew what was in man; the fickleness, the cruelty, the fleshliness, the time-serving. John Baptist, as we have before observed, doubted. But Jesus, just because He loved him, could only help him as He helped others; and then left him to form his conclusion for himself. Of all hard things He ever did, whether to Himself or His friends, the hardest must have been the message He sent back to Bethany, "This sickness is not unto death," and then His remaining where He was till His friend was in the grave and all hope had died out of the wondering sisters' soul. The love of Christ, as manifested in His earthly

Matt. xvii. 17.

John vi. 27.

John xi. 4.

ministry, is as a bright jewel, from many polished facets shedding its brilliancy on the world.

On the love of His atoning Passion I will not write very much now—we shall have to revert to it presently. But the death whereby He redeemed us is the summit and climax of that infinite pity which moved Him to atone for the world. "Greater love hath no man than this, that a man lay down his life for his friends." Nevertheless, "while we were yet sinners Christ died for us." We see it in the eagerness with which, on His last journey to Jerusalem, He went before them in the way and they were afraid. We see it in the awful, intense shrinking of His soul from the world's sin-bearing, when the full weight of what redemption implied fell upon His pure spirit, and for a moment He faltered and reeled. We see it in the washing of the disciples' feet, and in His trying at the very last moment to soften and save Judas. We see it in His warning to Peter before he denied Him, and in His look at him of sorrowful tenderness when he denied Him—the look that saved his soul. We see it in His silence and in His speaking; in

The Passion.

13.

Rom. v. 8.

His lofty prophecy of His return to judgment, the "blasphemy" that sealed His fate; in His mysterious announcement to Pilate that He was a king—an announcement indeed that could not restore the doomed captive—might have saved His wretched worldly judge. We see it in His words to the mourning women; in His prayer for His murderers, as in the first transport of indescribable anguish and shame, He looked down from the cross on the mocking, cruel throng. We see it in His welcome to the penitent malefactor, and in His last tender thought of His human mother. We see it in the sentence of triumph in which His parched lips proclaimed the fulfilment of His lifework, and in the final word with which He surrendered His spirit into His Father's care. The love of the cross is but the love of the entire life. The sacrifice of the cross only completed the sacrifice of Him Who in life had gone about doing good, and healing all that were oppressed of the devil; and Who in dying stripped him of his power. He Who when the cruel nails were about to be driven in, refused the myrrh, that nothing might dull His self-consciousness or rob Him of the rapture of suffering for men and of communing with God, at the end took the sponge of vinegar, and let them moisten His lips with it, that He might have strength for uttering the blessed word of victory, and before men and angels for confessing the Father of His love with unfaltering devotion.

To conclude. 1. The love of Christ is the love of two distinct natures in the one undivided personality of His incarnate being. As man, in the perfection of His human nature He had His preferences and friendships; sought sympathy from some more than others; permitted one, who was specially dear to Him, to lie on His breast at supper, and question Him as to who would betray Him; invited others, usually three, once four, to be with Him in the selected moments of power, or revelation, or distress; and as a man with a friend, solaced Himself with their company.

Christ's love the love of two distinct natures.

Is it presumption or irreverent to suppose that even now the Son of Man in heaven specially reveals Himself to, exceptionally delights Himself in, favoured and chosen souls? There are men and women—we all know them and admire them from afar—about whom we feel that they are more than others the sharers of His secrets and the possessors of His friendship; that in a sense they are the sacraments of His presence and grace to those who are in company with them; and that whenever we find them we seem to be entertaining angels unawares.

Of His Divine love—His love as God—this we know, that He is the Lamb slain from the foundation of the world. We seem to gaze down into it more closely, to approach it most nearly, when we ponder that last sacerdotal prayer: "I in them and Thou in me, that they may be made perfect in one; and that the world may know that Thou hast sent me, and hast loved them as Thou hast loved me."

<small>*John xvii. 23.*</small>

2. The love of Christ is a marvellous and unique combination of opposite and usually inconsistent qualities. There is "the love of Christ which passeth knowledge"; there is also what the beloved apostle elsewhere calls "the wrath of the Lamb." Both these aspects of love were exhibited in the human life of Jesus. To separate one from the other, or to contemplate one to the exclusion of the other, is to divide and dismember Christ. He

<small>*A combination of opposite qualities. Eph. iii. 19.*</small>

<small>*Rev. vi. 16.*</small>

was so gentle, yet so terrible; so tender and yet so strong; so patient and yet so capable of blazing into a very passion of righteous indignation; so considerate and yet so true. His love was in its idea, object, method, a holy love. It did not care only to please, or to gratify, or to soothe. It had also to do the work of the surgeon's knife and the physician's medicine; to show men themselves, not to deceive them; to wound, that it might afterwards heal. Without dispute the beloved, holy Lord constantly did, and said, and denied, or took away what in us with each other would inevitably have the look of grave unkindness—might even dissolve the close friendship of years. He put men to pain when He thought they needed to suffer. Smooth things, merely for the sake of smoothness, never left His lips. To the rich young man whom He loved, He would not make life or duty easier than his own safety and the Divine law permitted.

Christian reader, may not we in these somewhat effeminate days, when to speak of retribution is felt to be a kind of curt impoliteness, and to press holiness seems inconsistent with the modern notion of the mercy of God, be content to learn from Him Who is Love that Truth and Righteousness are the twin sisters of Mercy and Pardon? The sternest, and bravest, and most uncompromising of all teachers Who ever opened his lips in this world, was He who gave His life to save it. He Who said: "Come unto me all ye that are weary and heavy laden, and I will give you rest," also asked: "Ye serpents, ye generation of vipers, how can ye escape the damnation of hell?"

Matt. xi. 25.

Matt. xxiii. 33.

Severe.

3. For Christ's love, while it is full of patience and considerateness for the sinner who sincerely repents, is full of severity and condemnation for the sinner who only pretends to repent, or makes his outward repentance a cloak for the indulgence of his sin. He refused to quench the smoking flax, or to break the bruised reed. He sat down with publicans and sinners. He also said to the woman who was a sinner, "Thy faith hath saved thee: go in peace"; and to her who was surprised in the very act of sin, "Neither do I condemn thee: go and sin no more." But as to those who made the commandment

Luke vii. 50.

John viii. 11.

of God of none effect by their tradition; who turned God's gift of a Sabbath into a bondage and torture; who would not submit to God's righteousness because they preferred their own; and who so sinned against God that when they could not deny His marvellous works, they attributed them to the interference of the devil; He reproached them, denounced them, warned the people against them; shrank not from describing their proselytising as making men more the children of hell than they were themselves. These were the words of the meek, and lowly, and tender Jesus, and He spoke them in the deep purpose of His unspeakable love. If His words of flame would not melt the impenitence out of their seared hardness, they might deter, and alarm, and purify others. Of all terrible and hopeless conditions, the most terrible and hopeless, as Professor Mozley has reminded us, is that of those who turn their vices and sins into religious virtues. It was because Jesus loved with so true and holy a love that with strong and even impatient hands He continually strove to tear away from men's faces the delusions and self-deceit which so fatally hid from them the counsels and righteousness of God. Love, in one shape, persuades and invites; in another, rebukes and warns. But it is all love, and the same love, though with manifold voices and with diverse aspects. He who went about doing good, and delivering all that were oppressed with the devil, by all ways would save all. Sometimes He spoke of God as the bountiful, long-suffering, forgiving Father. At other times, when it was needed, and to those who needed it, He made all who listened to Him think of God as a consuming fire. And He is both—because He is Love.

Individual   Finally, this love to the world is also a love to the individual; and only to acknowledge its greatness without appropriating its salvation is out of our own lips to declare our condem-
Text.   nation. "Who loved me and gave Himself for me," writes the apostle; and He can love each of us, and did give Himself for each of us, because the Son of Man is also Son of God. My friends, we are not saved in a crowd, and we do not repent in a crowd. As single and separate souls we sin, as single and separate souls we must repent and believe and love.

Each of us must each for himself recognise his separateness, confess his sinfulness, believe his Gospel, accept his Saviour. "Every man shall bear his own burden"; but he can only bear it by taking it individually, consciously, penitently, trustfully to Him who loved, and died, and rose again for every one of us, and Who claims from each of us an answer to the question of questions— "Lovest thou me?"

Gal. vi. 5.

John xxi. 16.

ITS PURPOSE

" The highest attitude of any man's life is to stand waiting for what use God will choose to make of him."

Bp. Phillips Brooks.

II

ITS PURPOSE

"*He that hath seen me hath seen the Father.*"
JOHN xiv. 9.

THE universal, the insatiable, may we not say the sublime, necessity of mankind has been to know God. This necessity may spring from a sense of dependence, or from a dread of punishment; from a longing for goodness, or from a craving for light. But, be the cause what it may, men, as a whole, have never been content without a religion of some kind. Some religions, no doubt, can only be described as ghastly devil-worship; and others have expressed little more than the vilest human instincts materialised into foul divinities. It is true also that of the only two religions that seriously compete with the faith of Christ, one is too far above man to reach

Man's universal need.

him; the other too much below to edify him. Buddhism looks down upon him from the inaccessible heights of an arrogant self-effacement. Mohammedanism insidiously bribes him with a paradise of gratified lusts. It remains nevertheless a fact that all the religions of the world have been in a real sense seeking after God; and all its philosophies, experiments more or less successfully aimed at finding Him. The everlasting moan of the race has been, "Who will show us any good?" and if melancholy, it is reasonable. While some have not scrupled to go so far as to say that all the religions before Christ have been "sincere and age-long prayers for light," the truest expression of the most enlightened desire is the sentence of Philip, "Lord show us the Father, and it sufficeth us." To this question, on our Lord's own showing, the one complete answer is the Incarnation. "He that hath seen me hath seen the Father."

The claim of Christ—and it is an unspeakably lofty one—is that He reveals God. To see Christ is to see God in the closest and tenderest and deepest of relationships—that of Father. If you ever want to know what God would think, or feel, or say, or do, or order, or bestow, or deny under any given circumstances, look into the Gospels, and let Christ give the answer. The sum of it is this: God in Himself, and by the reason as well as by the senses undiscoverable, is to be seen and known only in His Son." "No man hath *John i. 18.* seen God at any time. The only begotten Son, which is in the bosom of the Father, He hath declared Him." Let us now ponder Christ's love in its eternal and magnificent purpose.

To put it otherwise, what did He mean by it? How did He set Himself to accomplish it? How is it an example for us?

The purpose of His love, that which because *A fourfold purpose.* He loved He desired to do, that also which He did, and could only have done, by and through the energy of love, which conceived and willed and accomplished it, was fourfold: to reveal the Father; to destroy the works of the devil; to make reconciliation for sin; to gather together all things into one in Himself.

I. The first aim of His love was to reveal *To reveal the Father.* the Father, for the glory of the Father, and thereby for the illumination of the world. In revealing the Father, Christ reveals His love, His power, His holiness. We should have never known the greatest of revelations to the world, that God is love, but for Christ; Whom God in His love and because of it, gave, sent, tried, surrendered, and then glorified. "Herein is love, not that we loved God, but that He loved us, and sent His Son to be the propitiation for our sins."

1 John iv. 10.

The love of God may be described as a love of benevolence and a love of complacency. Benevolence in its general purpose and universal providence; complacency in its personal delight and spiritual fellowship.

The Incarnation, with all that came from it, is the expression by Christ of the Divine benevolence in God's love to the world.

The personal and Divine inhabitation of the regenerate soul is the satisfaction of the Divine complacency in God's love to His Church.

John iii. 16.

"God so loved the world that He gave His only begotten Son." Here is the original and supreme and universal benevolence of God.

John xiv. 23.

"If any man love me he will keep my words, and my Father will love him; and we will come unto him, and make our abode with him." Here is His personal and holy and special complacency over the Church. We shall refer again to Christ's love more than once, and in fuller detail, and not without some unavoidable repetition. We will not further dwell on it now.

Christ's love again reveals God in His power —power ever wisely exercised for men's highest welfare.

The attribute of almightiness is perhaps that one under which the human consciousness most commonly apprehends God. It has its awful as well as its consoling side; and when even Christian teachers, with the best intentions, have described God as if He were just one of themselves, only infinitely stronger, this conception of His power has, even in the quarters where we should least have expected it, done grave mischief. Power by itself may be the worst kind of weakness, and so mean no more than the opportunity for a vindictive tyranny. When moved by love, and directed by wisdom and working for holiness, it is the mightiest thing that exists. Christ's miracles, on which we have touched already, are an exemplification of the mighty power of God; and this, the Gospels tell us, the people recognised them to be. In the spontaneousness and yet self-restraint, in the deliberateness and yet facility,

C

in the tenderness and yet the solemnity, in the majesty and yet the simplicity with which He wrought them, we see Him going in and out among men, the living, speaking Epistle of the attribute of His Father's power.

In His wisdom He revealed the Father as love. Two things we notice of Him Who in the Old Testament Scriptures was foreshadowed as the wisdom of God.

One is that, though He never claimed advice, yet, out of kindness to His disciples, He more than once invited them to explain what under certain circumstances it was best for them to do. The other is, that as His one object was to teach, and comfort, and save men, not merely to add to their responsibilities, and aggravate their doom by telling them what they could not apprehend, or giving them what they could not use, He imparted His heavenly doctrines only and when they were able to bear it. Perhaps His almost first object was to reveal the holiness of God; that His Father's purpose in sending Him, His own purpose in coming when sent, was to redeem us from all iniquity, and to purify unto Himself a peculiar people zealous of good works. His entire conscious life was a progressive manifestation of the righteous character of God, and of His longsuffering patience, and of his abhorrence of evil, and finally of His everlasting purpose to found a kingdom of saints. "Be ye therefore per- *Matt. v. 48* fect, even as your Father which is in heaven is perfect," was Christ's message to men, exemplified and embodied in every least action of His life. Another secret of His purpose was to destroy the works of the devil, which are sin, pain, and death. How He destroys sin we shall see presently. "He is the propitia- *1 John ii. 2.* tion for our sins." He destroyed pain, partly by showing us how to interpret, and endure, and use, and even welcome it; partly by translating us into a life to come, where there shall be no more pain, nor crying, nor tears. He destroyed death, by taking away the fear of death, and trampling it under His feet. "He *John xi. 26.* that liveth and believeth in me shall never die." Another purpose of His love was to make reconciliation for sin. In a single sentence the two crucial facts of the world's history have been summed up—man has sinned and Christ has died. St. Paul thus describes it: "All things are of God, Who hath reconciled us to Himself by Jesus Christ, and hath given to us the ministry of reconciliation, to wit, that God was, in Christ, reconciling the world unto Himself, not imputing their trespasses unto them." What sin cost God and Christ and humanity, we need be God or Christ quite to know. Only eternity can reveal the unspeakable woe of it, if unforgiven; the unspeakable gladness of being finally delivered from it, when we see the Lamb that was slain, and cast our crowns before the throne on which He reigns as Saviour and King.

No mind of sinful man can in the least conceive what it must have been for the holy Lord Jesus Christ to live day by day in a fallen world, to breathe the atmosphere, to hear the language, to endure the scoffs, to feel the impenitence of sinners; and then, at last, to experience in His inmost spirit what His holy Father felt about it; and as the world's sin-bearer, to bend under the burden of the world's guilt resting on Him, its representative and head, in all its unspeakable horror. But it was in love that He offered Himself to bear it; in love that He endured daily the contradiction of sinners against Himself; in love that He felt a kind of ineffable gladness in being made sin for us, if we might be made the righteousness of God in Him; in love that He could at last say, for our sakes, even more than for His own, "It is finished." Once more, it was the purpose of His love to be the predestined and supreme centre, in which the Father's will should be accomplished by the gathering together of all things in one—both which are in heaven and which are on earth, even in Him; that in His incarnate person the final aim and end of the Eternal, the Fatherly Wisdom might be completed by the summing up, as in a head, the works of His hands and the thoughts of His wisdom, and the fruits of His redemption, and His final and irreversible triumph over sin and death. No doubt it is all a mystery; but a mystery is something which we, if imperfectly, yet really see; not something of which we can see nothing. We are told just enough to understand that God's ways will thereby be completely vindicated before the universe, and that Christ, as the Head of His Church, and the Lord of nature, and the Captain of the angelic hosts, will in Himself at once declare and glorify and sustain the

John xix. 30.

creatures of His hand, and the spoils of His cross, and the organs of His providence, and the ministers of His power; Himself love—uniting and preserving them in love; His unspeakable reward, that the Divine purpose has triumphed; His holy fruition and gladness, that by love, and all that it implies, He has destroyed, and for ever, the works of the devil.

Men spin their theories, and the sparse and scattered hints which occasionally gleam on us out of the Bible are imprudently and often unreasonably pieced together into a web of almost arrogant doctrine, which will not bear the strain of a child's questions. The Church has suffered, and souls have been troubled, and God's Word has been made answerable for what it never uttered, or meant to utter; and God's silence—so merciful, so wise, so inexorable—has been peremptorily disregarded, almost violated. Nevertheless, behind all these things the eternal Word lives and rules, waits and loves. It is as if we stood on a hilltop and saw a vast plain at our feet, wrapped up in a silver mist, yet not so impenetrably as altogether to conceal the plain, while dense enough to hide what is moving on its surface.

In Christ all things are to be reconciled, and summed up and joined, and invested with an immortal glory. In Christ, Whose infinite love has made it both possible and actual; in Christ, at once the word, and the organ, and the channel of the Love of God.

II. Once more, God is love; and the life of Christ on earth, as the Gospels tell it to us, is the visible and historic, and predestined expression of its meaning and fruitfulness for man. *Its meaning for man.*

When we see how the Son of Man at His heavenly Father's hands accepted the circumstances which environed Him, welcomed the discipline which educated Him, encountered the hindrances which impeded Him, and interpreted the trials which afflicted Him, we too are to learn how the sons of men, following in His steps, and rejoicing in His fellowship, and expecting His return, are to live and work, and suffer and trust, like Him.

The Father loved the Son with a love which the human mind can neither imagine nor describe. Because of that love, in the fulness of time "He sent forth His Son, made of a woman, that we might receive the adoption of sons." *Gal. iv. 4, 5.*

How was His love shown?

That human life, as the Holy Spirit has inspired men to write of it, escaped none of the troubles with which we are familiar; enjoyed none of the immunities for which we, not too wisely, sigh; faced all the problems which struggle and poverty and want bring daily home to the hearths of the millions of the world; and included all the experiences which were needed to acquaint Him with the trials of the race.

Let us look into this for a moment, or we shall miss the pass-key to God's own dealings with ourselves, and lose one of the chief lights which illuminate the mystery of His providence. The temptation in the wilderness is, of course, the prominent, if not the greatest, example of the spirit in which, as St. Paul in one place writes, "verily, Christ pleased not Himself."

Rom. xv. 3.

He would not turn stones into bread to satisfy an innocent and exhausting hunger. Nor would He, by a sign from heaven, which more than any other was likely to have seized the imagination and impressed the senses of the multitude, make an easy road for Himself to the suffrages of Israel, by descending, on the wings of ministering angels, from the pinnacle of the Temple into the courts below.

As the ministry went on, He steadily refused to make life easier or smoother for Himself, when a look or a word would have done it. "Foxes have holes and birds of the air have nests, but the Son of Man hath not where to lay his head." He borrowed a fishing-boat of one apostle, and shelter from another. When He crossed the sea between two deeds of mercy, He did not forbid the storm to rage over Him as He slept, though to comfort the disciples in their alarm He sternly bade it be still. On another occasion, as if to show them that He was Lord alike of earth and sea, He walked upon the water as upon dry land. The same power which healed Malchus might have struck His eager enemies dead at His feet.

Luke ix. 58.

There are indeed now and then to be observed in His life and ministry sudden and brief flashes of His eternal glory—acts and words for a definite and saving purpose, which may be not inexactly expressed as the occasional exercise of the Divine attributes, which as a rule He declined to exercise. When He suddenly passes through the angry crowd, whether at Nazareth or in the Temple; when He calmly predicts for His apostles' instruction the fact of His coming Passion, though in the ministration of His earthly life He permitted to be hidden from Him the day when the world would be summoned to judgment; when He holds lofty communion with His Father the hour before He passes to His cross; when, smitten by His majesty, the soldiers who a moment after bound Him, fell at His feet, as if overpowered by His glory—we see He was Eternal God as well as a creature born of a woman; we also see that to Him no personal advantage came of it, except that it helped Him to teach and to aid those whom He yearned to save.

Assuredly, it is a sublime and yet a touching lesson that true love is absolutely disinterested; does not claim as a reward for duty, or as the price of devotion, ease, comfort, success, or honour. The gifts and capacities with which God endows us are trusts to be used for His glory, are possessions to be shared with His creatures. The example of Christ, the incarnation of Christ, the cross of Christ, all proclaim the lofty if the hard gospel of constant sacrifice.

Selfishness is the one thing which Christ cannot permit, or endure, or condone. If the daily cross-bearing is the rule of the Christian's duty, love makes the yoke easy and the burden light.

III. God is love; and as the love of Christ was the manifestation of the Father to the world, so our love to each other is to be the manifestation of Christ. Herein we have fellowship with Him, both in purpose and spirit and activity, shining as reflected lights of Him Who is the Light of the World; and continuing in a lesser, yet a real, sense His work of redeeming mankind. "Let this mind be in you which was also in Christ Jesus." The Church is to be the living epistle and witness of Christ; the Church as a body, and the Church in each of its members; and this is best done, because most intelligibly, through love. St. Paul bids us walk in love, as Christ also loved us and gave Himself for us.

Our love to each other to manifest Christ.

Phil. ii. 5.

What does it mean to walk in love? Three things: to hold the truth in love, which is the secret of controversy for the faith; to put on charity, which is the bond of perfectness; to count it more blessed to give than to receive, which is the way of helping the world.

Controversy. Not all men are fit for controversy, nor are they all called to it. The gifts which equip and enable for it are important and possessed by but a few. Too often it happens that where there is the capacity and knowledge and the intellectual keenness, the zeal that sharpens the sword is zeal for self, not for God. The victory desired and snatched at, instead of defending the Church from outside enemies, only divides her against herself. To contend earnestly for the faith once delivered to the saints, is one of the primary duties. Without her champions in days long past the Church would have ceased to exist. The gates of hell would presently have robbed her of her creeds, which would mean to have robbed her of her life. But earnestly must also be sincerely, kindly, generously, humbly, as a witness for the whole truth, and not only for our own fragment of it, with brethren whom God teaches and we should respect, not as with enemies whom Satan inspires and God denounces. No men do more useful or needful or blessed service for the Church and the Church's Master than those who, by learning and argument, explain, and defend, and harmonise the great truths of our most holy faith; but it must be done with the purpose of winning, not crushing; with the motive of exalting Christ, not magnifying self. Christ had His controversies, and His apostles after Him; and often His blessed spirit waxed eager and hot, and even indignant. He wondered at the slowness of His own disciples, and reproached it. When the Pharisees rejected Him, He scrupled not to indicate the true cause of it: "How can ye believe which receive honour one from another, and seek not the honour which cometh from God only?" Nay, when some men stumbled at His deepest and most startling doctrine, so far from withdrawing it or explaining it away, He repeated it, and traced their murmuring to the lack of spiritual intelligence: "The words that I speak unto you they are spirit and they are life. But there are some of you which believe not." But it was not to win Himself glory as a teacher. He attributed all He said to Him Who sent Him: "My doctrine is not mine, but his that sent *John v. 44.*

John vi. 63.

John vii. 16.

me." It was simply because He loved men that He longed to win them into the truth, and, when they rejected it, He warned them. Flatteries of polite speech never characterised Christ. Yet there was nothing in Him of an arrogant or militant egotism. "The whole experience of Christian life must be a growth in the apprehension and certainty of Christian truth." But to declare truth, as those who hold it in love, is a secret the Church needs to learn just now.

Professor Loberley.

To "put on charity which is the bond of perfectness" is Christ's secret for society, and one special feature of it, which St. Paul takes care to indicate, is the forbearing and forgiving between man and man. "The bond of perfectness" means, I suppose, that which fastens, and keeps fastened, the various perfections which make the soul's holiness complete. Without charity there would be nothing to cement them into one organic life. The expression of charity is kindness; the test of charity is forbearance; the beauty of charity is tenderness; the crown of charity is forgiveness. To be kind ought never to be hard. To forbear means self-restraint, the

ol. iii. 14.

first condition of manhood. To be tender is
a grace of disposition, into which rougher and
more austere natures need a good deal of
disciplining. Home and its charities, sorrow
and its lessons, sickness and its humiliations,
are the Divine medicine here. But forgiveness
is sometimes not only the hardest but the most
perplexing of all. What must we forgive?
when must we forgive? and why must we
forgive? For it is clear that a too facile and
quick forgiveness with baser natures only
tempts them yet further to presume. It is
no kindness to them, it is no benefit to
society, it is no honour to God, it is no pro-
tection for oneself, to treat grave offences as
though they did not matter. We remember
that the Lord said, when the apostle asked
him about it, "If he trespass against thee *Luke xvii.*
seven times in a day, and seven times in *4.*
a day turn again to thee, saying, I repent,
thou shalt forgive him." And while we
do not wonder that the apostle immediately replied, "Lord, increase our faith," *Ver. 5.*
we observe, we ought to observe, that
the forgiveness is only enjoined when the
repentance is expressed, and when we may

rightly infer that the repentance is proved to be sincere.

Christ laid down three great lessons on this subject, pointed by His own example and teaching. He forgave Peter, for his tears showed his repentance; and He prayed for him even before the denial, that his faith might not fail him. He forgave His murderers, and, as the natural result of it, prayed His Father to forgive them. "They know not what they do," was His claim on His Father's mercy. As St. Paul afterwards explained about his own persecution of the Church, they did it "ignorantly in unbelief." But He could not forgive the Pharisees, for they hardened their hearts against light and truth and the Spirit of God. He could not forgive Judas, though to the last He tried to soften and so save him, by washing his feet, and sending him the sop which was to do him honour. The disposition to forgive is what God expects and desires, when the time comes for bestowing it: "Let not the sun go down on your wrath" is always a duty for all men at all times.

Luke xxiii. 34.

1 Tim. i. 13.

Eph. iv. 26.

Acts. xx. 35.

To count it "more blessed to give than to receive" is the sentence of Christ; and it is a paradox at which the world scoffs, though it is the Church's law. Here, too, we have the providence of the Father to guide us—the example of Christ, and the secret whisper of the regenerate soul. God makes no distinction in the bounties of His love or in the principles of His government: "He maketh the sun to rise on the evil and on the good, and sendeth the rain on the just and on the unjust." So Christ, in the dispensing of His supernatural mercy, healed all that were brought to him, on the one condition that they had faith. Faith was absolutely indispensable as man's receptive faculty of good. *Matt. v. 45.*

Christ only asked one question, "Canst thou believe?" We need only ask one question, if it is in our power to help, "Art thou my neighbour?" with a wide range for that large word.

IV. Once more, let us clearly understand and ever remember that, as the purpose of Christ's love to us—and of His Father's, in and by him—was in the fullest sense a moral purpose, not to make us happy in the world's sense of the word, but to make us blessed; not to screen us from trouble, but to deliver us from evil; not to train us for the eternal life by softness and sunshine, but to brace and nerve us for that self-restraint and self-denial which are the essentials of Christian manhood: so our truest and deepest way of showing love to each other—a Divine love—be they children, or friends, or neighbours, or the world outside, is not by always saying yes, or by a quick response to the moods and caprices of the hour, or by a facile sympathy with fantastic sorrow, or by even a too great readiness to deliver the back of burdens which God has laid on it, meaning it to carry them, or by a hurry to administer anodynes when the true safety of the spirit may be in enduring a little wholesome pain.

There may be a dangerous softness and petting in the way in which we endeavour, meaning well, to soften the burdens or soothe the anguish of life. We cannot love too much, but let us love wisely and thoughtfully. If God does not always answer our prayers the moment we utter them—and this is in no lack of love, rather in the excess of His love to us—it may not always be expedient for us to do it with each other.

The world needs tenderness, I know; but

the world also needs discipline. We are to be strong as well as kind, prudent as well as pitiful. Society at this moment, at least that part of it which has benevolent instincts (not indeed too large a part of it), seems to be in danger of a mawkish and caressing philanthropy, which is by no means the Divine way of stimulating mankind to rise on its feet and exert itself, from which sagacious persons, who can think as well as feel, portend real danger to our social system before another generation has passed. To be wiser than God, holier than God, kinder than God, no one would consciously strive to be. Yet this, some of us are unconsciously trying to be. We must bear each other's burdens, but there is one burden which each man must bear for himself, and bear alone—the burden of his own being. We must walk in love, and have our words and acts, and consents and refusals, and protests and rebukes, and controversies and struggles, bathed in it, so that no word of bitterness, or venom, or conscious injustice should needlessly and unjustly wound one soul for which Christ died. We, like Christ before us, are to be ready to "bear the infirmities of the weak, and not to please ourselves." We, *Rom. xv 1.*

like St. Paul before us (it is a great mystery which only love can fathom, and a vast burden which only love can accept), are even to rejoice in our sufferings for each other (whatever they mean and however they come) if only thereby we fill up that which is behind of the afflictions of Christ in our flesh, for His body's sake, which is the Church. The more that love goes out from us into the world, the more love will be poured into us from God; and the reward of human love, so sweet when we get it—we do not get it too often—will be surpassed only by the sense of Christ's love—sweeter than honey and the honeycomb.

But, I repeat it, though we do not need less kindness, we do need more wisdom. It is good to love, it is also good to think. Christ's nature all moved together.* It would be good if ours moved more together. The end of the Incarnation was the re-uniting of man to God; and the fruits of it are to be the Divine nature regenerating and transfiguring humanity. "Honour all men; love the brotherhood," was St. Peter's precept. "Ye have an unction from the Holy One, and know all things," was the assurance of St. John.

Pet. ii. 7.
John ii. 0.

* I am indebted for this thought to Bishop Phillips Brooks.

ITS METHODS

"There is a sign which outsoars all other miracles, and only grows more wonderful as the ages pass along, and that is the empire of Jesus Christ over human hearts."

REV. J. R. ILLINGWORTH.

III

ITS METHODS

> "*And I, if I be lifted up from the earth, will draw all men unto me.*"—JOHN xii. 32.

THIS was a startling promise, and none the less startling for the explanation which followed. But for that explanation, we might reasonably have referred it to that crowning moment when, having spoiled principalities and powers, and trampled under His feet Death and Hades, Christ ascended up on high to lead captivity captive, and be the Priest upon His throne. St. John, however, almost hastens to make this interpretation impossible. It is true that Death could not hold Him—that He died that He might rise, and that He rose that He might take possession of His kingdom. But it is not glory here that the Lord is thinking of, it is shame; it is not the welcome of angels, but their holy and wondering tears; it is not deliverance from those who had no pity, but the climax of the ineffable anguish which He suffered at their hands. The song of the drunkard, and the mocking of the priests, and the gambling of the soldiers, and the cold stare of the crowd were full in His mind. Yet He also foresaw and foretold the triumph out of them; when, for the joy set before Him, the shame and the agony seemed of but little moment; when, made perfect through suffering, He was also to conquer by it; and so the middle cross with its wounded and quivering burden was to become the most potent force the world has ever seen, upon the mind and heart of mankind. "I, if I be lifted up from the earth, will draw all men unto me." "This He said," adds the apostle (in the manner we elsewhere observe in him), "signifying what death He should die."

Ver. 33.

Christ's love, in the power whereby it asserts its existence, and achieves its triumph, and retains its dominion, shall be our contemplation now.

It is a subject about which every regenerate heart has its own abundant and separate experience; it is also one which, while it touches the deepest chords of human feeling, and heals conscience as no other remedy can heal it, profoundly affects the entire spiritual being of man, and is vital to the solution of some of the grandest problems in Christian philosophy.

We will consider the sphere of this Divine method, or where it operates; the varieties of it, or how it operates; the instruments of it, or what puts it into motion. Behind and above the subject of our contemplation ever seems to stand the awful, blessed cross with the Sin-bearer hanging on it. If His death was the supreme and culminating manifestation of the love which was at once the nature and purpose of Him "who loved us and gave Himself for us," it is also the master-power which alone can turn the "rock into a standing water, and the flint into a fountain of waters." *Ps. cxiv. 8.*

I. The sphere in which this redeeming love operates is fourfold: that of mind, and conscience, and heart, and will. We begin with the mind, for the mind is at once the avenue and the council-chamber of the soul; the avenue by which facts, and ideas, and opinions pass on into the invisible laboratory, where they take shape and life, or wither and disappear; the council-chamber, where the sifting, and the pondering, and balancing are more or less instinctively and rapidly transacted, and where the final mental result becomes an essential factor in the volition and activity which follow. For in proportion as the mind loves truth will it consent to apprehend it, and even have joy in apprehending it. It is a noble and inspiring love, which will never rest contented in the truths themselves, but will pass on to Him Who reveals them. When, for instance, setting ourselves to think out this amazing love of Jesus of Nazareth, we speculate on its cause, examine its history, deplore its requital, debate its object, the question occurs—Can there be a loftier one? Why did He love those with whom He had so little in common, and about whom an apostle writes, "While we were yet sinners Christ died for us," whether we consider the stock from which they sprang, or the race of which they were an obscure, if ineradicable offshoot? In a word, what was there in man as a race, or the Jews as a nation, to deserve the sacrifices He made? There is but

Rom. v. 8.

one answer to this question; and though it is insufficient, is there any other? He loved us because it so pleased Him. It pleased Him because He was the Son of God; and God is Love.

The moral infancy and inexperience in which our forefathers found themselves in paradise were presently and miserably exchanged for a knowledge of sin, which displeased God, but did not finally alienate Him. The fallen child was still loved; though fallen, he was a child still. Out of love to him he could yet no longer be treated as if he had not fallen. While man could not, out of very hope for his recovery, be protected from or at once delivered out of the manifold consequences of his abused freedom, the love that had fashioned, and blessed, and spared him, instantly and deliberately promised his salvation; and tenderly, through a long series of ages, expected his return. That return was effected through the Incarnation, and in that satisfaction, or propitiation, which, as the two profoundest of the inspired thinkers, St. Paul and St. John, explain to us, were the fruits of that love which humbled itself for man, and, partaking of his nature, lived, obeyed, suffered in it, to make reconciliation with God, and bring in an everlasting righteousness. No doubt there are mysteries here connected with Christ's atonement for sin, and the Divine acceptance of it as an essential satisfaction to Eternal Righteousness, which baffle the keenest intellect, when attempting to penetrate them; and about which our safety and our blessedness is to accept and adore. But we can at least see that they are mysteries; and we may stand on the brink of the abyss and reverently look down into it, even if we cannot fathom its depth. The human mind, when it knows its limitations and accepts them, will not arrogantly claim, whether in revelation or in physics, to grasp or to comprehend all truths presented to it. Here, and about all things, "we know in part, and we prophesy in part." What it may and should claim is that nothing should be presented to it contrary to reason, and therefore contrary to God; not that nothing should transcend reason. To know what we can and what we cannot see is the wisdom which is at once dutiful and reasonable.

1 Cor. xiii. 9.

> "*Strong Son of God, immortal Love,*
> *Whom we that have not seen Thy face,*
> *By faith, and faith alone, embrace,*
> *Believing where we cannot prove.*"

In Memoriam.

There is no faith that is not based on knowledge, and there is no knowledge of God possible apart from faith. As God loves the whole of man, whom He has made that He might love him, and whom, when He had made him, He pronounced to be very good; his body, which He has clothed with such dignity and beauty; and his will, by which His supremacy is recognised and obeyed; and his conscience, where even now He judges on His throne, and his heart which He claims, possesses, and beatifies with His presence; so He loves his mind, which He has fashioned and ordered with its laws and its capacities, and its limitations, its pure delight, and its lofty ambitions; and the thinker, knowing that he is judged, and thought of, and cared for, gladly receives into the inmost depths of his mind the light and fire of Divine love, which acts as summer-time on its activities, germinating, stimulating, fertilising, maturing them, and accepts the magnificent trust of revelation as a treasure never to be exhausted, as a mystery never to be explored.

On the conscience this love of Christ works with an awful yet softening power; and it works through the cross. Was it only the priests who sent Him to His Passion; only the fickle crowd that shouted, "We will not have this man, but Barabbas"; only Pilate, in whom the thought of two worlds fiercely, if briefly, contended, and over whom the present world gained the mastery; only the soldiers, who mocked Him with the reed, and the purple, and the crown? Had our sins no share in that mighty and unique tragedy of lovely and majestic innocence, yielding itself to shame and death to put away guilt and bring in righteousness; with the shedding of that blood in which there is redemption, even forgiveness, have we had nothing to do? As He hangs there we are drawn to Him, for He beckons us to His feet. He has no reproaches for us, only a silent appeal against a hard impenitence. He has no request to us except to come to Him, just as we are, that He may give us rest. His cross smites us, and yet His cross heals us. We feel that there must be a holy wrath at sin, or why is Jesus there, bruised for our offences and stricken for our iniquities? But we also

John xviii. 40.

feel that the wrath is a righteous wrath, and that God could not be God if He did not feel it. We also recognise that there is forgiveness with Him, not through our merit, but through His pity. Jesus who prays, and saves, and mourns, and dies on that cross, prays, saves, mourns, and dies because God is Father, and He is the Son of His love, and the love which provides the remedy persuades the repentance, and the cry of our heart drawn to Him in His humility and anguish goes up to Him:

> "*Rock of Ages, cleft for me,*   *Toplady.*
> *Let me hide myself in Thee.*"

But when the conscience is smitten and healed, the heart burns, burns as with a consuming fire. Nothing conquers like love; and there is no love under the sun so potent, so wonderful, so tender, so beautiful as the love of the dying Jesus. Those blessed arms, stretched out on the limbs of the cross, seem to embrace the world in their grasp. The very attitude seems to say, "Because I love you, I am dying for you. I am dying for you because my death will deliver you from the most crushing burden and from the most implacable tyranny, and from the most depressing fear. All I ask of you in return is to know and believe my love; is to claim and accept my salvation; is to see in my cross and my agony my Father's love and my Father's holiness; most of all, to learn to hate sin as He hates it; to understand about me that "greater love hath no man than this, that he lay down his life for his friends."

John xv. 13.

When, then, the mind is instructed, and the conscience stirred, and the heart on fire, the will moves, umpire and sovereign of all. Christ recognised this in Himself, as the Son of Man, when, in reply to the leper's prayer, "If Thou wilt, Thou canst make me clean," He said, "I will, be thou clean." He recognised it in us when He solemnly complained to the Pharisees, "Ye will not come to me that ye might have life." The will is only then completely mastered and won when it has been approached and persuaded by all the other organs of our spiritual being, acting according to their nature and in their order. But when we look at the cross, the glory of which the mind has apprehended, the salvation in which the conscience has welcomed, the love of which the heart has accepted—then it is

Matt. viii. 2, 3.

John v. 40.

ripe and safe forthwith to choose and to obey. Then, and then only, "the love of Christ constraineth us; because we thus judge that, if one died for all, then all died: and that He died for all that they which live should not henceforth live unto themselves, but unto Him which died for them, and rose again." *2 Cor. v. 14, 15.*

II. The varieties of this method, or how it operates, are chiefly didactic, and exemplary, and sacramental, and corrective.

By didactic I mean (something has already been written of it) the story of the Saviour's love as it is set forth in the Gospels, which, in its simplicity and disinterestedness, tenderness and humility, has no parallel in the record of any other human life, and was utterly beyond the imagination of man to create. The fact of its being described by those who could not have described it if they had not seen it, is an absolute proof of its being true. A superficial knowledge of this history will, indeed, do no more towards melting or winning the soul than a winter's sun on an iceberg. It must be pondered and meditated in the heart if it is to penetrate it, and to transfigure it into the beauty it portrays. There are few more potent helps to holiness than meditation; and there are few who think, where there are thousands who feel.

The exemplary method is that of the power of the saintly life, whether read of in a book, or present to the senses, or known of in the world. For man has a mighty charm over his fellow-man; and a saintly soul can be, in a real way, a means of grace to the Church; and the love of Christ, when it enters, and transfuses, and glorifies a human spirit, shines out of it like a flashing splendour, glows forth from it with warmth and heat to light and fire the soul. To see how others love Jesus, and what that love helps them to do, and suffer, and resign, stirs us to inquire into their secret, and to covet their blessedness. We feel that love can be caught, and stirred, and fed. He Who loves them, loves us also. Will He not visit us, too, and make our joy full?

And this exemplary method works quietly and almost unconsciously; it is hardly aware of itself; it does not lift up its voice in the streets; it does not covet admiration, and it is frightened by praise. It is ever with a sense even of sin and imperfectness, though also of acceptance and filial liberty, that it walks in the light as God is in the light. It cannot understand how others are helped by it; its secret amazement is that it is so thin and shallow and poor.

The sacramental method is that whereby, by effectual signs and seals, the grace of God is conveyed to the devout soul, and therewith and thereby the fulness of the love that passeth knowledge. It is, indeed, a bald and ceremonial and even degrading view of baptism only to regard it as a sort of formal registration into ecclesiastical privileges, and not to see in it a wonderful instance of God's love in freely and ungrudgingly incorporating us into the society of His redeemed family, whereby we have the right to call Him Father, and constantly to claim at His hands the supply of all the needs that a creature can feel, and the expression of all the love that God can bestow.

The ordinance is not less precious to those of us who recognise infant baptism as agreeable to the mind of Christ, and in analogy with the institution of the first covenant. Let us remember that the Lord, Who loved children as well as men, Who took them up in His arms, put His hands on them, and blessed them, Himself took on Him the helplessness and infirmity of infancy and childhood, that every age of man might recognise in Him, Who called Himself Son of Man, the brotherliness that is only born from experience.

In the Holy Communion of the Body and Blood of Christ we see the supreme manifestation of the love of Him Who died that we might live, Who loved that we might love; in it and from it we may expect and may claim the gift, and the fruition of it. "This do in remembrance of me," is a command which touches duty with pathos.

Luke xxii. 19.

Christ asks to be remembered, for our love is precious to Him. In this way of remembering Him we learn that He, too, remembers us, when He imparts strength, and renews pardon, and ripens activity. If He does not seem worthy of our love when we come to receive what is the memorial and channel of it, when will He seem worthy? If He will be slow to give us the sense of His love, in its freeness, in its unchangeableness, in its unutterable sweetness and beauty; why does He welcome us to His banqueting-house only to send us empty away? The gift is there for us; it must not be hazarded or forfeited to sincere souls through the infirmity of a morbid subjectiveness. He who knows what is in man, for He shares the nature which He Himself made and gave, is in no such hurry to halve our blessing or to chill our joy.

"By sacraments men are to be taken out of the narrowness and isolation of their own lives, out of all engrossing preoccupation with their own state, into the ample air, the generous gladness, the unselfish hope of the city of God; they are to escape from all daily pettiness, all morbid self-interest, all preposterous conviction of their own importance, into a fellowship which spans all ages and all lands." *Dean Paget* We need not vaguely hope that we may somehow receive His grace; for He has told us where and how we are to find it, and what are the conditions of its unhindered entrance into our souls.

There is also the disciplinary method—for some men, perhaps for all, the only one, both of revealing the unutterable tenderness of God and of opening our hearts to receive it. We should never comprehend the awful holiness of God but for the consequences of sin, which defies and violates it; we should never even taste in all its wonderful sweetness of the love of God, but for pain. In this disciplinary method, to which our Lord Himself was no stranger, for He learned obedience through the things which He suffered, there are three chief elements — Death, Pain, Darkness. When, however, we speak of them as disciplinary— that is, as implying an educating method for filling us with the love of God, a word of careful explanation must be premised. They are disciplinary in the sense of their being used by God, not as ordained by Him. For there is good reason to suppose that they are neither features of His purpose, nor elements of His government, nor ordinances of His will. Rather, they are invasions and interruptions of our life; disappointments and stumbling-blocks in our path. Death, as we know it, is "the wages of sin," not the primal thought of God. Pain, so far as we know, though God's medicine and surgery, as He uses it when it appears, was no original thought of His (so far as man is concerned, at least), for the creature which He made in His own

Romans vi. 23.

image, to share His unspeakable bliss. Darkness, whether intellectual or spiritual, is utterly and essentially alien to Him Who, in the beginning of creation, said, "Let there be light"; and the gladness of Whose Divine nature it is to reveal Himself to the world. *Genesis i. 3.*

Of all these things we may truly say, not only that the Creator has never pronounced them good, but that, so far from being reconciled to their presence or continuance, He sent His Son to banish and destroy them for ever. As has been acutely observed, we lay on God's love a heavier burden than it can bear when, in consoling men under the awful sorrows of life, we lightly and conventionally attribute them to the act of God, rather than to the malice of Satan. It is an unspeakable mystery, but our Lord, again and again, in language neither of figure nor tradition, has attributed both disease and insanity to the intervention of the Evil One. While it is perfectly accurate to say that "whom the Lord loveth He chasteneth, and scourgeth every son whom He receiveth," it is equally accurate to affirm of all these mighty woes which fill our sad world *Hebrews xii. 6.*

with anguish, lamentation, and woe: "An enemy," not a Father, "hath done this!"

Matt. xiii. 28.

Death is a tutor for us all in the schooling of the love of Jesus. While nothing quite apart from our own interest in it so forcibly strikes the moral imagination as the spectacle of Christ dying for the world, which at once despised and destroyed Him; so nothing so forcibly or continuously impresses the awfulness of our mortality, the solitariness of our personal existence, the responsibility which no one can share, the dissolution which nothing can postpone. Hour by hour it is coming to meet us; everything else is uncertain—the place, the time, the shape in which it will come. That it will come we may forget, but we cannot deny. In that supreme moment to be able to fall back on Him Who has tasted death for us, because He loved us more than His own life, and Who has taken away both the fear and the sting, and the loneliness of it, because He has passed through it and conquered it, has died for our sins, and risen again for our justification—what a blessed peace this, and what a noble hope! In that hour He will stand by us, and say, "Fear not,

ITS METHODS

for I am with thee." The love that endured death and triumphed over it, will then steal into our souls, and help us as we pass to see His face and catch His smile. *Isaiah xliii. 5.*

To take but one instance: pain, about which one writer has said that "it is the deepest thing in the world"; and another, that, even more than knowledge, "pain is power"; is sometimes flung at Christians as a fact utterly incompatible with the idea of the goodness of God, often also by Christians, and by believers before Christ, hastily interpreted as the consequence of personal sin. That much of the physical pain which mankind endures is the result of the violation of natural laws, whether inherited or otherwise, is true, and in that sense He Who, in His own wisdom, framed those laws, and at once warned and guarded men from disobeying them by painful consequences, may be said to be its ultimate cause. But the death upon the cross, with its unspeakable sorrow, so utterly dissociated from personal sinfulness, and the Incarnate life on earth, with the disappointments, and rejections, and misunderstandings, and opposition it stirred, should be enough to teach *Prebendary Eyton* *Rev. J. R. Illingworth.*

us how to dissociate sin from suffering. As His pain, borne so patiently and joyfully for us, draws us to Him with an irresistible attraction, we must not forget that it also involves us in the duty of taking our share in that solemn but magnificent sacrifice by which, as St. Paul said, we "fill up that which is behind of the afflictions of Christ in my flesh, for His body's sake, which is the Church."

<small>Col. i. 24. Quoted already. See p. 52.</small>

Pain unites us to each other, who are all members of a groaning and travailing and mortal family; it also unites us to God, Who helps us to say, "The cup which my Father hath given me, shall I not drink it?" It is even possible, as some of us know, to comfort ourselves and to glorify God in our pain, by sincerely and humbly thanking Him for it. Arnold, when he was dying in mortal agony, blessed God out of a true heart. When the promise is breathed into the quivering spirit, "My grace is sufficient for thee," the peace comes to us which the world can neither give nor take away.

<small>John xviii. 11.</small>

<small>2 Cor. xii. 9.</small>

Darkness, whether intellectual or spiritual, is a grievous pain; and the malice of the

Evil One, acting on the nervous system of an enfeebled body, may succeed for a time in shutting out from the soul the light and face of God. Whether it is doubt of the existence of God, or of His justice, whether it is a sense of sin, incompatible with a hope of salvation, or a conviction of failure which fastens down the soul into a gloomy despair, God is lost, and the supreme trial of the saints, only to be understood by those who have passed through it, stings and burns with fire. Some of us may have it behind them; others may have it in front of them; in either case it is a discipline for the love of God. Jesus felt it when He was redeeming the world; and Jesus can enter into it now. It need not be a mark of displeasure, though it must be a crisis for faith. Here, too, the steadfast soul, which can see in the darkness and trust in the silence, knowing in Whom it has believed, will suffer and wait. The patience and faith of the saints mean in the end so much greater capacity for the love and service of God. "Who shall separate me from the love of Christ?" is the thought which stills the soul into a perfect calm.

Romans viii. 35.

III. Once more, there is the Divine instrument of this method; only one, God the Holy Ghost. If teachers would remember this with their pupils, and parents with their children, and pastors with their flocks, the Church would have a new life given to her, and we should be no longer asking, "Why art thou cast down, O my soul, and why art thou disquieted within me?" It is God the Holy Ghost Who takes of the things of Christ, and shows them to us; Who opens our eyes that we may understand them with obedience and welcome them with joy; Who convicts us of sin, and then points us to the Sin-bearer; Who shows us the majesty and beauty and necessity of righteousness, and then unites us to Him Who was made sin for us that we might be made the righteousness of God in Him. This is the dispensation of the Spirit. It is to be wished that we felt it more. What the angel said to Joshua he says also to us: "Get thee up; wherefore liest thou thus on thy face?" If you want to love Jesus, ask Jesus to show you how He loves you, and He will answer you by the gift of the Holy Ghost. It is His blessed work to shed abroad the love of God in our hearts;

Psalm xlii. 5.

Joshua vii. 10.

it is His only — there is no other. We shall never stir or deepen our own love by lamenting its littleness, or by feebly desiring its growth. "We love Him because He loved us"—and to learn to love is to begin to pray. *1 John iv. 19.*

In conclusion, we are to see the marvellous power of sacrifice. It is a truth which again and again forces itself as we meditate on the redeeming love, at the very moment of its apparent failure. Something of its value for us, apart from the personal share we claim in its magnificent triumph, is that it must be for us also, in all our efforts for others, to enjoy and hold fast the eternal life. Christ on His part can only own and use and bless us just so far as we take His yoke upon us and learn of Him; and His yoke is the spirit of self-sacrifice. Men will only be drawn to us, and believe in us, and yield themselves to our persuasion, so far as they perceive that we are sincere in really desiring their good, and prove it by our denying ourselves for their sakes. We succeed as we deserve; and it is love that deserves, and the blessed reward of being loved is that men listen to us as we speak of Jesus, and seem to recognise this voice in ours.

Then it is a personal Christ to which each separate soul must go for life and peace and duty. There are two great truths, equally vital and indispensable: the one the individual salvation, the other the corporate life. The individual salvation means the separate, conscious, intelligent cleaving of the personal soul to the personal Lord.

To *me*, Jesus says; not to an orthodox creed, not to a divine society, not to an inspired book, but to Me. "I, if I be lifted up from the earth, will draw all men unto *me*." And so elsewhere He is careful to emphasise, both when He invites and when He condemns, "Come unto *me* all ye that labour and are heavy laden, and I will give you rest." This has gone down from age to age, with its ineffable and tender music, to be the solace of millions whose hearts knew their own bitterness, and no stranger intermeddled with their joy. What do I know personally of the Saviour Christ—of what He has done for me, and of what He claims from me? Have I in any sense a personal knowledge of Him, such as a man has of his friend? Did He shed His blood for me, and have I asked

Text.

Matt. xi. 28.

Him to wash me into perfect whiteness? Has He earned salvation for me; not only from the punishment of sin, which is, perhaps, the least part of its consequences, but from its guilt and from its power? And can I in any sense say, "I know on Whom I have believed, and am per- suaded that He is able to keep that which I have committed unto Him against that day"? When I see Him as He is, seated on the throne of His glory, shall I recognise in Him one Whom I have worshipped, and trusted, and served, and followed, and loved, and wished for; or will He be a stranger, Whom I never wished or tried to reach or win upon earth, and Who can only have one sentence to say to me—those supreme words, "I never knew you"? (Matt. vii. 23.) *2 Tim. i. 12.*

Christ has His limitations. "If ye believe not that I am He, ye shall die in your sins." And He will not force men to believe. Faith is an act of the will as well as of the understanding. To force the will would be to take from man his moral freedom; and were such a thing possible, the love of God would be in conflict with the righteousness of God. There could be no judgment if the judged were not *John viii. 24.*

Text. free. "I, if I be lifted up from the earth, will *draw* all men unto me." Has it drawn you? Reader, the love of Christ, manifested on the cross, is a real, a precious, a free gift to you. What will you do with it? Will you accept it, and let it save you; will you reject it, and make it condemn you in the irresistible and unquenchable memory of a lost and self-reproaching soul?

ITS CLAIMS

*Man has no right to take his full rights
in the world."*

Bp. PHILLIPS BROOKS.

IV

ITS CLAIMS

"*Whosoever he be of you that forsaketh not all that he hath, he cannot be my disciple.*"—LUKE xiv. 33.

CHRIST, assuredly, did not make things too easy for His disciples. Three times in this one discourse is this tremendous sentence repeated: "He cannot be my disciple"; each time with a condition of discipleship sterner and harder than before. Hating our life, carrying our cross, forsaking all we have —why, claims like these, we should have thought, would have earned either a bitter resentment or a silent disdain from most men but for two circumstances—separately attractive, together invincible—His sincerity and His worthiness. He meant what He said, and He merited what He claimed. That He was true, down to the very depths of His being, true with a truthfulness to which His own life bore constant testimony, was transparent to all. What He asked them to do for Him, He was already doing for them, with this added, that behind His demands were His promises, and that His promises anticipated, fulfilled, surpassed all that they could imagine or desire. Were they weary? let them come to Him for rest. Were they in darkness? He was the Light of the World, let them hasten to stand in it. Were they sinful? He was to give His life a ransom for many. Were they hungering for something to satisfy their deepest spiritual longings? He was the Bread of Life; if they came to Him they should never hunger; if they believed on Him they should never thirst. And surely the best proof of their conviction of His intense sincerity is in the fact that immediately after this discourse, so full of hard sayings, and solemn warnings, and lofty claims, and penetrating appeals, we read: "Then drew near unto Him all the publicans and sinners for to hear Him." They understood Him—it was impossible not to understand Him; and instead of resenting His plainness, they flocked to His feet.

Luke xv. 1.

But it was not only respect for His courage that drew them, it was the attraction of His love. All this He said to them because His love to them was so deep, so holy, so complete. To make religion smooth, and facile, and pleasant, would not have helped them much; it would only have added one more to the world's hypocrisies. Because He loved them, He made these mighty claims on their faith and loyalty. Because He loved them, He would help them to understand, from the first, that it was goodness, not prosperity, He desired for them: and goodness could come to them only in one way.

"Whosoever he be of you that forsaketh *Text.* not all that he hath, he cannot be my disciple." The claims of Christ's love we are to consider now, in the penetrating splendour of the central thought of the text that those claims can only be met by us, and satisfied for Him, through the wondrous method of sacrifice.

I. *His claims.*

The first in order, as well as in importance, *Acceptance.* is that we accept Him; and accept Him with something more than the baptismal incorporation which others have procured for us; or than an intellectual assent which need have no moral quality going with it; or than a conventional profession, which may be simply a homage to propriety; or than a hope of final salvation, which may sometimes be a kind of selfish baseness. He does not, indeed, wait for us to come to Him. He knows us too well for that. He comes to us. The strayed sheep may or may not miss the shepherd's care and the shelter of the fold; it is the shepherd who must go after the sheep which is lost, until he find it. "Behold, I stand at the door and knock. If any man hear my voice, and open the door, I will come in unto him, and sup with him, and he with me."

Rev. iii. 20.

It is the will that lays hold of Christ, the personal will cleaving to the personal Lord. The mind may have its conception of His glory and the conscience may tremble at His holiness, and the heart throb with the sense of His tenderness. But until the will is yielded there is no vital, actual union between the soul and Christ, and He will not force the will. He can only appeal to it, and help it. He comes to the door of the soul and knocks at it. Have

See p. 54.

not you heard Him knocking at yours? You know you have. But the door must be opened from within, and it is the will that opens it. When the will opens it, Jesus comes in, to be Saviour, and King, and Master.

But "whosoever forsaketh not all that he hath" (whatever it may be, whatever it may cost), "cannot be my disciple." Unless Jesus is felt to be worth everything, practically He is worth nothing. He cannot share the temple of the soul with any idol. His honour and our salvation are at stake.

He claims docility. A disciple is one who *Docility.* learns, and the sort of disciple that Jesus cares for is the disciple who is ready to sit at His feet and hear His word; to surrender prejudice, however stubborn, and to unlearn error, however dear, and to accept doctrine, however strange, if only it is clear that He imparts it. In giving love, He bestows truth—quite the best thing love can give; and He claims in proof of love that His words be humbly and gladly received, for they are the Father's words, and, being spirit and life, they must be spiritually discerned through the teaching of the Holy Ghost. No greater honour can be done to the claims of Christ, and no better test of the reality of our love to Him, than by the intelligent study of His Holy Word. But I am not sure if this honour is very much given to Him, or that this text might with safety be very frequently applied. His Word is the organ of His will, the mirror of His nature, the voice of His fellowship, the channel of His grace; and just so far as these things are dear and precious to us, shall we constantly and privately, and with a sense of delight, go to His Word for them. Nothing keeps our doctrinal system in such ripe proportion, or gives such real dignity to our spiritual consciousness, or such power to our confession of faith, or such help for deep repose to our inmost, deepest being, amid the cares and bustle of life, as communion with Christ in His Word, where mind and heart, intelligence and devotion, seek Him and find Him together. He has His special secrets for those who are at the pains to come and ask for them. And He not only teaches but comforts.

Psalm cxix. 165. "Great peace have they which love Thy law, and nothing shall offend them;" and it is because they love Him.

Imitation. Imitation is another thing His love claims

from us. "Take My yoke upon you and learn of me;" and unless the cross-bearing is in His steps, and following close behind Him, the cross will not be recognised as a cross, for He has not chosen it and fitted it to our shoulders; and what we call the imitation of Him may only be a specious and perilous egotism, the phantasm of our own self-love. What Christ meant by His yoke is most completely shown by the act of which I have already spoken, His washing of the disciples' feet the night before His Passion. "I am meek and lowly of heart," He said. "As I have loved you, that ye also should love one another." A wonderful book has been written on the imitation of Christ. Most of you will know it. Disfigured with a few small monastic conceits, here and there occasionally professing axioms of the religious life which the instinct of a robust faith pronounces to be extravagant, if not impossible, it has a hold on the spiritual respect of Christian people, for these two statements, beyond all others: that it teaches us that Christ deserves everything at our hands that we can possibly give Him; and that His love, stealing into the soul, makes heaven upon earth. Love, we

Matt. xi. 29.

John xiii. 34.

Thomas à Kempis.

mean, which is manifested in sacrifice, beautified by humility, yearning after holiness, welcoming sorrow, or loss, or pain, if only it may enjoy God's love. In a word, that mind which, as St. Paul tells us, was in Christ Jesus, and is to be reproduced in us, is that yoke which we are daily to carry on the neck of our stubborn wills, and thereby to convey to the world the presence of an unseen Saviour. To love one another for Christ's sake; to see and love Christ in one another; and to love Christ Himself supremely, increasingly, delightedly—if this is our aim, this will be our reward.

Service.
John xii. 26.

Christ claims service also, because He loves us and desires our highest good. "If any man serve me, let him follow me." This may mean, of course, that the first and best way of serving Christ is to imitate Him; and that no amount of benevolent activity can safely dispense with a consistent obedience. But surely it also means that, if we wish to serve Christ, we must not go before Him; we must come after Him. As Christ Himself ever did on earth, we must not so much choose our service as leave Him to choose it for us, waiting on His providence and expecting His command.

Christ Himself has defined what He means by His servants. "Ye are my friends if ye do whatsoever I command you." The acceptableness of our life, the dignity of our employments, the fruitfulness of our activities, and the secret of our peace are to be found not in any one way of life as distinguished from another, or in any calling (save one, perhaps), as specially earning the favour and benediction of God. The one aim of our daily activity, whatever it be, should be to recognise God in it, as our bountiful and overruling Father, Christ as our Master and Lord, the Holy Ghost as our counsellor, and sanctifier, and guide; whatever we do, doing it heartily as unto the Lord, and not unto men; doing it also gratefully, in the name of the Lord Jesus, giving thanks to God and the Father by Him. This in olden time gave the Christian slave self-respect, and inspired the magistrate with justice; it makes the sword in the soldier's hand the weapon of the Lord of Hosts; it reminds the merchant in his daily affairs that a man's life consisteth not in the abundance of the things which he possesseth; the statesman will think of Daniel, who three times a day knelt in prayer to God,

John xv. 14.

and imitate him; the physician at the bedside will bring with him the presence and blessing of the Son of Man, who Himself "took our infirmities and bare our sicknesses."

Matt. viii. 16.

He claims our faith. "What I do thou knowest not now, but thou shalt know hereafter."

Faith. John xiii. 7.

When the Lord said that to Simon Peter, He felt that He had a right to be trusted, and He was hurt that the claim was not instantly recognised without the necessity of making it.

When the Lord says it to us—and He often has to say it in lonely and clouded hours—the plea that goes with it is, "Think how I love thee, and what I have done to deserve to be trusted: wait till the light comes, and the shadows flee away."

Christ claims on the ground of His infinite love to be trusted about everything—about body and soul, about time and eternity; about salvation and holiness, about usefulness and duty.

When children disappoint us, or friends forget us; when death shadows the home, or sickness corrodes the health; when disappointment robs life of its spring, and duty of its gladness; or when changes, that undermine and destroy all we really care for, remove the very landmarks of our life; when, most and worst of all, the Face that smiles on us our salvation is hidden from us, and the Love of the Everlasting Father seems to our darkened and bruised spirits to be exchanged for a holy awful silence at the weight of guilt resting unrepented on our soul, it is not so easy to reply, as those who have never wept under the anguish would say—to reply, "Though He slay me, yet will I trust in Him." We do not fear the dark when there is light gleaming into it; we do not dread the storm when Jesus is in the vessel, though He be asleep. But to lose Him, with the sense of His presence, the shining of His face, the murmur of His voice, the touch of His mercy-seat—that makes the soul reel under its awful desolateness. "If God be with us, who can be against us?" That we understand; that we all can say! But to be separated from the love of Christ is an anguish which makes devout and tender souls tremble with misery.

Job. xiii. 15.

Rom. viii. 31.

Still He says, "Trust me." Still we must

try to cling to Him; and to be sure that He never dies, never changes, never forgets, never forsakes.

From His own parched lips there once rose to heaven a cry which has reached the conscience of the world: "My God, my God, why hast Thou forsaken me?" Sometimes His saints now, whom He loves most tenderly, and uses most honourably, and disciplines most constantly, are called to pass into the darkness of His veiled presence and His closed lips, that, in their darkness and woefulness, they may manifest to those who stand by that they know in Whom they have believed; and that the highest pinnacle of the spiritual life is not happy joy in unbroken sunshine, but absolute and undoubting trust in the love of God.

Matt. xxvii. 46.

II. *The need of decision about them.—* Christ comes to us and claims our love, and bids us decide, for there is no such thing as serving two masters at once. "He that is not with me is against me;" and the time is short. At all times it is surely reasonable that we should see just where we are as we travel towards eternity—that we should judge ourselves while yet there is time. Consider the

Matt. xii. 30.

reasonableness of Christ's claim. He has created us, and He has redeemed us. He emptied Himself of His glory for us; He drank to the very dregs the cup of pain, and shame, and desolateness, and rejection, that in and for humanity He might vindicate the awful righteousness of a holy God, and be made sin for us, that we might be made the righteousness of God in Him. Can we refuse Him what He asks of us—that which, if it is His glory to claim, is our blessedness to give? If we refuse it, what reason can we give for refusing it? If we grant it, does any one doubt it will have a full reward? There are various ways of treating it, but the feeblest and most perilous of all is the indecision which thinks to postpone, but actually refuses; which puts Him off lest He should prove a great disappointment, and prefers to keep this present evil world, as something of which, at least, we may be sure. Some listen to Him— they know He loves them—but the cross is too heavy and the burden too great; they are really sorry, but it seems impossible; they have had one glimpse of Paradise, but they will not go in; its gates close, and they go away. Others come to Him, and try Him for awhile, but persecution, or affliction, or severe duty, or intolerable sacrifice intervene, and they are offended, and walk no more with Him. Others accept Him, and, not without infirmity and shortcoming, are true to the end. And then their joy—how full, how sweet it will be! If we have not yet closed with Christ, let us close with Him now. If we have not yet laid our life at His feet, let us lay it at His feet now. If we have never really opened all our heart to the fruition of His unspeakable love, let us open it now. Of two things very wonderful, one is perhaps more wonderful than the other, also more shameful. It must be wonderful to the angels in heaven and the lost spirits in darkness that so many should despise and postpone the salvation and the love of the Lord Who bought them. But, I suppose, more wonderful still and harder of explanation is it that those who love Him a little should not come to love Him with a more consuming, and absorbing, and constraining love; and that when He has been so gracious to them as to forgive them, and bless them with His forgiving mercy, they should be coldly satisfied with their supposed immunity from punishment, should requite Him, not with their love laid joyfully at His feet, but with a circumspect devotion and a measured service. "Whosoever he be of you that forsaketh not all that he hath, he cannot be my disciple." *Luke xiv. 33.*

Let us further notice how significant is the admonition of the Lord following instantly on the absolute necessity of entire self-sacrifice— *The need of entire self-sacrifice.* "Salt is good: but if the salt have lost his savour, wherewith then shall it be seasoned?" *v. 34.* The inference is indisputable. The salt of the Christian life is sacrifice, and if the spirit of sacrifice die out of it, and the essence of that spirit, which is love, become chilled, and its activities and devotions presently diminish, and decay, and disappear, the salt of the life is gone, and its growth paralysed, and its influence killed, and its testimony silenced. "Thou hast a name that thou livest, and art dead": *Rev. iii. 1.* "repent and do the first works," is the Lord's message to that soul. His pleading with it— *Rev. ii. 5.* "Hast thou got weary of me, and art thou disappointed in me?"—presently loses all its tender sharpness. The bane of the Church of God, the dishonour of Christ, the laughing-stock of the world, is in that far too numerous body of half-alive Christians who choose their own cross, and shape their own standard, and regulate their own sacrifices, and measure their own devotions; whose cross is very unlike the Saviour's, whose standard is not that of as much holiness as they can attain, but of as little holiness as they can safely be content with to be saved; whose sacrifices do not deprive them from one year's end to another of a single comfort, or even a real luxury, and whose devotions never make their dull hearts burn with love of Christ. Oh! let us examine ourselves under this picture, often true if humbling; and let us each ask ourselves what we are doing, and enduring, and sparing, and sacrificing for our Lord and His Church. Are our neighbours better for us? Is the spirit of our family, in any sense, permeated with the sincerity of our religion? Are we moving on in deepened penitence, and enlarged benevolence, and quickened devotion, to the vision and welcome of our King; or are we, not consciously perhaps, but actually, trying the most unworthy, and also the most perilous experiment that the human soul can try—of being scarcely let in at the risk of being just left out? "Whoever he be of you that forsaketh not all that he hath, he cannot be my disciple." *Text.*

The last lesson that needs to be pressed—and it shall be full of consolation—is the sufficiency of grace.

Let us frankly, readily confess that this saying about forsaking all that we have as an essential condition of discipleship is a hard saying, and who can hear it? Of course, in the primitive time it came very close indeed to the personal experience of the Church, and had its awful fulfilment in bonds and agony and blood. We in our soft times shrink from trials and duties, which to the martyrs were a sort of alleviation of the tragic possibilities of their lives. It is also true, that though we may be ready to forsake all that we have for Christ's sake, it does not follow that Christ will put His ordinance into complete or sudden execution; what He expects is that we should be invited and ready to surrender all to His will. But it remains true that the law of complete self-surrender is absolute, and with *The sufficiency of grace.*

no exception, and with no appeal, and that it may mean any day for any of us tasks which are exhausting, and sacrifices which are impoverishing, and losses which darken our home, and calamities which hasten us into decay. We are to be ready, and even willing, for them. Like the servant waiting for his Lord, and expecting His instructions, we ask ourselves, "Who is sufficient for these things?" and the answer comes back, "My grace is sufficient for thee; for my strength is made perfect in weakness."

2 Cor. ii. 16.

So once more we meditate on the blessed, inexhaustible, sustaining, exhilarating truth of the love of Christ. That love is bountiful; it is also righteous. It is very holy, and it is very real. In every duty there is strength when the duty is actually present, though not an hour before. For every sacrifice there is joy, deep-hidden, sweet, but not till the voice is heard, "Come, take up the cross and follow me." For every parting, when the moment comes (have not we found it so?) there is a strength and a calmness and a faith given, which has eyes for the gates of Paradise, as they open for our loved ones to pass in, ears

2 Cor. xii. 9.

Mark. x. 21.

for the harpers on their harps as the new song is being sung, to give them their greeting as they pass into the city. Death seems transfigured into life, and becomes a vivid reality, as Jesus whispers, "I have the keys of hell and of death," *Rev. i. 18.* and so the greatest of sorrows, which we cannot share, or pass on, or pretend to make light of, have even their healing in the thought of the sympathy of Jesus, and in the unfailing promise—can we hear it too often? —that "all things work together for good to them that love God." *Rom. viii. 28.*

There is a great secret here; let me try to tell it. *A great secret.* This grace of God, on which a man relies, must be a perpetual element in which his life abides, and not an occasional assistant and supernumerary called in, "when it is suddenly or specially needed." *Bishop Phillips Brooks.* And this love of Christ of which we have been speaking is not to be locked up, like a cordial, in a sealed casket, hid away till it is wanted, and then suddenly taken out and put in all its strange lusciousness to the white and fevered lips. It is to be the daily, hourly atmosphere of our entire existence and consciousness, in which we go to our duties, and endure our trials, and meet our conflicts, and offer our devotion; as the breath we breathe, and the lesson we know; the one truth, which is absolutely without dispute, and the one treasure which man can neither give nor take away. Christ loves us with an everlasting love, and He loves us, not to cast us off or to overwhelm us, but to honour us by duty and to elevate us by sacrifice. There is everything in Him for us that we can want, and His wise way of teaching us this is to deepen our sense of dependence, and make more close, more vital, more blessed the union of our souls with His. He does not desire self-completeness for us; as it has been beautifully observed, we must not want it for ourselves. What is best for us, and best for Him, is that everlasting childhood which will also be the condition of our glorified life in heaven, where He will still lead us, still feed us, and still be our light, still be our King. But for this end all walls of separation must be broken down between us, and He has His own way for breaking them down; so that the light, and grace, and love, and joy, and liberty and devotion flow from His life into our life, by the channels, ordinances, works, and dispensations He is pleased to use; and so His joy becomes our strength, and His service perfect freedom, and His love a blessed and growing reality, and His image an increasing eternal great reward; and we cease to wonder and tremble at the great claim in the text, "Whosoever forsaketh not all that he hath cannot be my disciple." For we have begun to learn the greatest of all lessons, the secret of all good, that when we love, and as we love, His yoke is easy and His burden light.

ITS BLESSEDNESS

> "*I long to enjoy Thee in my inmost soul, but
> I cannot lay hold on Thee.*"
>
> THOMAS À KEMPIS.

V

ITS BLESSEDNESS

" To know the love of Christ, which passeth knowledge.'
EPHESIANS iii. 19.

A PARADOX is an indispensable commonplace, which universal assent is wont to environ with the subtle peril of being either despised or forgotten, and which prudent teachers will continually impress on their disciples, if even in an eccentric and almost startling fashion. When the great apostle, who knew as much of his Master's love as any man, wrote to the Ephesians this sentence about it, having immediately before offered a prayer that they might know it, and own it as their greatest treasure, he was not conscious of any inconsistency; he simply wished to enforce on them that just because it surpassed the human mind to know all of it, therefore should they instantly set themselves to know as much of it as they could.

The "length" of it, if indeed we suppose (not too readily to be taken for granted) that the wonderful sentences immediately preceding the text refer to this love, and not to something else distinct from it, takes us back to the eternity behind time, and on to the eternity in front, when time shall be no longer. The "breadth" of it gives the universe, with its countless worlds, as the scope of its holy and majestic activities. The "depth" of it penetrates to the vast spirit world in Hades. The "height" of it lifts up the soul to the heavenly places, where to saints and angels is made known by the Church the manifold wisdom of God.

To know all of this love at any time, or to know it at once, or to know it easily and at will, is impossible. In this sense it is that the love of God passeth knowledge, for it is unfathomable and infinite, and not to be expressed in words.

But to know something of it at once, and to know more and more as life goes on, and all through the ages to come to be deepening in the knowledge of it, and gratefully to accept from day to day all the discipline that may help us to receive, and absorb, and transmit it to others—this is eternal life, in our Lord's meaning of it; this, in St. Paul's figure, is to be filled into all the fulness of God. On the blessedness of this love I must try to write now. How little it is that can be written, and how cold and feeble my writing must be.

"Eye hath not seen, nor ear heard, neither *1 Cor. ii. 9.* have entered into the heart of man the things which God hath prepared for them that love Him." But though they may be more than we are able to express, they are here; and God reveals them by His Spirit; and each man's personal experience is the only absolute proof of it to him. For I cannot know it for you; and you cannot learn it for me. I can only press on you that it is to be known; and that life is another thing when we do know it; and that we may each know as much of it as we please; and that so far as we know it, shall we be filled with God.

Let us consider some of the elements of this blessedness. *The elements of the blessedness.*

The love of Christ is a love *from all eternity.* He was the "Lamb slain from the foundation

<small>Rev. xiii. 8.</small>

of the world." In other words, if the inference is a fair one, when the world was to be made, the Son of God Who made it foresaw that man for whom it was made would need redemption as well as creation; that the redemption he would need could only be accomplished by the sacrifice of His own life as a creature and fellow; that nevertheless He made man, made him, as a Latin Father has not scrupled to say, that He might have the bliss of redeeming him; made and redeemed him, out of the fulness of His infinite love. When we think that Christ has always loved us, His goodness bewilders us, but it also gives us peace.

He knew all that we should be in our unworthiness of His love, and still He loved us. He has loved us in the distant past; and resolved to save us, not for works of righteousness that we should do, but for His mercy. The eternity of His love, and the sovereignty of it, are parallel truths which help to illuminate each other. "Chosen" "in Him, before the foundation of the world, that we should be holy and without blame before Him in love."

<small>Eph. i. 4.</small>

But the eternity of this love is matched in its blessedness only by its *unchangeableness*. This is a truth of the Old Testament, repeated and developed in the New.

"I the Lord change not, therefore ye sons of Jacob are not consumed," was the prophetic assurance. "Having loved His own which were in the world, He loved them unto the end," is the historical statement of St. John. "Who shall separate us from the love of Christ?" is the triumphant challenge of St. Paul. *Malachi iii. 6.*
John xiii. 1.
Romans viii. 35.

It is important to observe of all these passages, with reference to what is known in controversial theology as the final perseverance of the saints, that they bear exclusively on only one side of that truth—the objective fact of the Divine faithfulness—and do not touch, much less discuss, the other half of the problem—the awful capacity in man to sin against grace, and light, and love. "All that the Father giveth me shall come to me," "and no man is able to pluck them out of my Father's hand," is a truth on which we rest as the charter and ground of our salvation. But we have no promise for those who drop the cross, or fall into presumptuous sin, or weary of unrequited service, and go back, whether sorrowfully or eagerly, into the evil world. There is only one thing which can *John vi. 37, x. 29.*

separate us from the love of Christ. It is our own wilful, persevering, deliberate sin. So long as we hate sin and resist temptation, and receive grace and love duty, we are as safe in the everlasting arms that were once nailed to the cross, as if we were standing, without fault, before the throne of God. There is no caprice in the Father's purpose, there is no fickleness in the Saviour's love. He will not change; nay, let me be bold and say He cannot change. Why should He? God is love.

Another element in His love, and almost the most consoling of all, is *the spontaneity* of it. How often the true heart, self-reproaching just because it is true, is tormented by the doubt, born out of a sense of its own unworthiness, of the simple impossibility for the holy Saviour to love one so vile, so worthless as itself! The way of life is a narrow way indeed, lying between the two quicksands of presumption and despair; and, according to our individual nature and the circumstances which happen to us, the tempter tempts us to either one or the other. And either way is death. Well, no amount of self-introspection, and no experience of human infirmity will ever succeed in con-

This thought will be found elsewhere.

vincing a sincere heart that it is worthy of Christ's love, or that it could ever hope to be through the sacrifice of a thousand lives. If, then, I am told to know and believe the love of God to me, and yet can find no cause in myself why He should love me, where am I to look and what am I to do? The answer is—and it is the voice of the Father—"My child, look unto me and be saved. I love thee because my hands have made and fashioned thee; because thou art the thought of my will, and the object of my mercy, and the manifestation of my glory. I love thee because I have bought thee with the blood and the passion of my beloved Son. Know and believe it; and be at rest." The simple, mighty, incredible, yet absolute truth is this: God loves us, because it has so pleased Him; and there is no other account to give of it, reason and argue as we may. On the Eternal purpose, on the Incarnate life, on the accomplished sacrifice, on the final victory rest at once the motive of God's love, the fact of Christ's redemption, the assurance of our own place in the Father's house as children and heirs.

Another element in it, not without its shadow

of mystery, is *the scope of it.* "God so loved the world that He gave His only begotten Son." It is a very, very blessed thought to an unselfish Christian to contemplate the vastness and illimitableness of the redeeming purpose. It is an insoluble problem to reconcile the apparent failure of the method with the original magnificence of the plan. It also stirs in a timid heart, sensitive to its insignificance, the anxious fear of being utterly lost in such a vast concourse—as if too small for God to see, or too worthless for Christ to save. But the vastness of the scope is to stimulate the activities of Christian pity. "How shall they hear without a preacher, and how shall they preach unless they be sent?" Whatever other things God may do, He will never take from man his moral freedom, or relieve him from the responsibility of his relation to others. To the individual Christian, the incontrovertible and undeniable evidence of God's love to him is his baptism. To be a member of Christ, a child of God, an inheritor of the kingdom of heaven; and to be all these through the inscrutable providence of the Divine Sovereignty which chose him to it, while hundreds

John iii. 10.

Romans x. 14, 15.

of millions were left outside in the darkness, is a distinct proof of love, which should silence and shame all querulous carpings about the direction of God's mercy—should say to him, in the apostle's words, "All are yours, and ye are Christ's, and Christ is God's." *1 Cor. iii. 22, 23.*

For, in immediate connection with the scope of the Divine love, and a concurring feature of its blessedness, is its *individuality*. St. Paul again and again asserts it in special application to himself: "Who loved me, and gave Himself for me." *Gal. ii. 20.* The historical evidence of it we possess in St. John, who always describes himself as "the disciple whom Jesus loved"; *John xxi. 20.* and in the account of the family of Bethany, of whom the Evangelist records, "Now Jesus *John xi. 5.* loved Martha, and Mary, and Lazarus." Let us confess that it is hard to appreciate the separate personal love of the Saviour to each individual soul. Reason may inflexibly decline to accept it; and, but for the instinct that compels to prayer, and the experience which recognises that prayer is answered, the thought of the heart, that it is known and cared for by God, might well be scouted as the dream of a presumptuous and silly egotism. But the corporate life of the entire society, and the separate personality of each individual member of it, are essential to each other as the only complete account of the spiritual condition of mankind. "Bear ye one another's burdens"— and "every man shall bear his own burden," are the two poles of Christian fellowship and personal responsibility. Christian readers, to each of you I dare to say, I rejoice to say, in the name of Him to Whom all hearts are open, and from Whom no secrets are hid—that Christ loves you with a separate, and individual, and complete, and discriminating love, as if there were no other being in the universe on whom His love could rest; that He loves you in spite of your unworthiness, and your insignificance, and unprofitableness, and self-reproaches; that He did not begin to love you because you were good, but because He wished to make you good; He did not love you because you were doing so much for Him, but because He meant to bid you and help you to try. The only thing He hates is insincerity. He cannot go on loving you if you are false to Him. The only barrier to His grace and your own blessing is a stumbling and faltering faith.

Margin notes: See p. 87 and passim. — Gal. vi. 25.

One other feature in the blessedness of Christ's love, and one which comes very near home to many of us, is its *tenderness*. The sentence in the Gospels which has, perhaps, touched more pulses in the moral temperament of mankind than any, is a sentence of two words, " Jesus wept." Tenderness is love in expression ; and the mere fact that such pains are taken to make it expressive at once accentuates the earnestness of the purpose to show it, and opens the depths of the heart to receive it. Instantly we admit that not always, or at first, was the Lord tender to those whom He most sincerely loved and most distinctly purposed to aid. Occasionally His manner was abrupt, and His questions incisive, and His conditions hard, and His delay painful. He dreaded effeminacy in the spiritual life; He never flattered, or pampered, or caressed ; and He refused to protect by anodynes from sharp but wholesome pain, those who He saw needed it. Yet all that came from the greatness of the love which filled His spirit, and from the skill and insight wherewith He would stimulate and ripen the soul for what was coming afterwards. Between man and man there is a felt affectation

John xi. 35.

See p. 40.

in unctuous expressions of feeling, which in the nature of things cannot always have much substance in them; there is also the risk of insincerity in a nature which always seems to stand at the pinnacle of emotional expression. Parents, moreover, who are always fondling their children with immoderate and uncalled-for caresses, are training them into an inevitable indifference. But when the occasion arises for tenderness, the affection will instantly and abundantly manifest itself; and so between Christ and the soul which He would heal, or comfort, or strengthen, the love which passeth knowledge has hidden ways and voices of its own.

I know it, and you know it. "It is I, be not afraid," comes to us out of the darkness.

Though a whisper, it is heard through the wrath of the tempest and the whiteness of the tossing sea. When sickness weakens and humbles us—and sickness is no charm for sanctity—if we trust Him and cleave to Him, we shall wait, and suffer, and listen, and love, and be still. Our tears move His pity; and our pain comes to us as a way of sharing His cross.

When the last enemy draws near, his insolence is stilled, and his javelin blunted; he is become but the messenger to the Father's House; the echo of a voice, as of the music of many waters, "Come up hither."

The tenderness of God—Oh, what words can adequately describe it; none can know it but those who have needed it and tasted it for themselves. To all of you who read these words I say: if you do not need it now, the day will come when you will need it. When flesh and heart fail; when the strength ebbs and the eyes grow dim; when the world is passing and eternity is nearing; when you can hear the plashing of the waves and the murmur of the new song comes sweetly and gently over the water; you will feel a face bending over you, to comfort as one whom his mother comforteth, to soothe as a friend who has gone through it all for your sake, and knows what it is: when you will discover, as you cannot discover now, the immense tenderness of the Divine Pity.

The sense of this blessedness of the love of Christ will of course vary both in the amount of it, and in the vividness of it, and in the occasion of it, with the temperament of the individual nature, and the processes of its spiritual discipline, and the eternal purpose of God.

Some will need more of it and some less; and the same person may need more of it at one time than another; more at one stage of life than another.

The mental constitution has its changes and epochs, as the bodily has. While some may need it often, others may need it seldom, and God gives it as He sees the need, not as we see it. When strong natures do need it, He gives it them; for sorrow in such souls is something terrible, and when expressed in tears, makes one even tremble. From others, where the temptation is to be emotional, and to rely on their sense of God rather than on His character, it is often withholden—kindly withholden. We are to walk by faith, not by sight, and feeling indulged may mean manhood weakened. Until we go to see the King in His beauty, we must not murmur if sometimes we enter the cloud, and even abide there. He is there with us, though we see Him not. The self-respect of Christian men will not ask for sweetmeats; it is content with bread.

There is, however, a time when the love of the Lord Jesus is specially needed to console and refresh the heart. The years draw nigh which have no pleasure in them. The body is humbled by sickness. The mind has no longer its eager and impetuous delight in books, or talk, or art, or music. The will does not leap at new activities; it is jaded by the diligence of the filled years, perhaps hurt and disappointed by the wreckage all round it of hope and plans and beginnings of the eager heart, now far in the hazy past. The conscience has its accumulating burden of unfulfilled tasks and dismal shortcomings, and of self put before God, and of sin which has stirred only a shallow penitence. The heart, dulled in its sensibilities, and wounded by the constant losses of friends going down to the grave with none to take their place, is apt to settle down into a moody indolence, or into a chronic discontent. At such moments, moments which we must all have observed and mourned over in others, which some day others may observe and mourn over in us—the one thing to do is to fall back, like tired children, on the thought of the unchangeableness of

Christ's love, and to be assured that, however little we deserve it, however feebly we may enjoy it, it is here, and here for us. It is such an awful sin, with Calvary in the far distance, for one moment to doubt the boundless love of God. Of that sin—that sin of sins—may we never be guilty; may our last years be full of fruitfulness through patience of suffering, and brightness of temper, and steadfastness of devotion, and immovableness of faith! If He hide His face from us, still we will trust Him. If He smile on us, and bring summer into our heart, we will praise Him, for light is pleasant to the soul. If He send us pain, we will not ask Him to remove it, if that might be to lose an opportunity for glorifying Him, but we may and we will ask for strength to bear it.

John Keble.

"*O Lord my God, do Thou Thy holy will,
I will lie still.*"

The blessedness of Christ's love helps us in another way, and a way likely to be more and more needed by reverent and yet intelligent Christians—reverent in their simple, dutiful loyalty to the written Word of God, as the authoritative expression of His Government,

His Being, His Character; intelligent in their clear perception that in some respects the Bible must be treated as any other book must be treated—as to the history and relations of its several books, and the period of their compilation, and the language in which they have been written. For not only is it the duty and the privilege of competent scholars thoroughly and courageously to study them, but the admitted result of their studies is not to be resented as presumptuous, but to be accepted as edifying; lest we find ourselves resting our salvation on a theory of inspiration, not on the Person of Jesus Christ; and lest in our beautiful fear that the honour of God should be violated, we forget to trust Him as the way and the truth and the life. Ours are times when everything seems to be in a condition of transition and flux; when the interpretations and expositions inherited from our forefathers are daily percolated and undermined by the relentless investigations of even devout scholars. We know and feel that God's Word continueth for ever in heaven; but we are jealous, and we ought to be jealous, of losing one jot or one tittle of that really Divine inheritance, the knowledge and possession of which is eternal life.

Here, as it seems to me, my brethren, the blessedness of the love of Christ steals into the soul, to give it safety and anchorage amid the tumult and disquiet all around it; and so we say, Why art thou cast down, O my soul, why art thou disquieted within thee? "Heaven and earth shall pass away; but my words shall not pass away."

Matt. xxiv. 35.

The secret of our peace and confidence is a threefold one—in justice and patience and love. Let us be just to these scholars, whose gifts and erudition and opportunities call them to one of the most honourable tasks a man's will can accept—that of studying and examining the text and the history of the Scriptures. Let us neither resent the scope of their inquiry, nor discourage the thoroughness of their investigations, nor fear the end of their research. They have their task, and we have ours. We will leave them with God, Who long ago moved holy men to indite these books, and Who also helps holy men to interpret them. For ourselves we will wait—only being careful to wait long enough. There is as much weakness in a facile and eager acceptance of insufficient though honestly-worked results, as there is self-will in resisting and rejecting what is with sufficient agreement admitted to be really proved, merely because it means something for us to unlearn. There is such a thing as a just scepticism, which both purifies and widens and illuminates and protects religion. We will hold fast the faithful word as it has been taught, careful only to know that it is the faithful word, and not a gloss of it; thankful also to remember that never was there a period, since the canon of Scripture was closed, when scholarship had a more complete apparatus of textual, and doctrinal, and historical helps than in these latter times of ours. For whatever else may go, Christ cannot go. In some of the Old Testament Scriptures, which Christ said testify of Him, and to which He constantly referred as a Divine authority, the final result of accomplished and laborious investigation may ultimately modify some of the convictions and positions held by us now, just as a generation ago our fathers were constrained to admit that the Book of Genesis was not a technical handbook of geology. The Church has survived that discovery, and will survive others. Do not fear, but love, and love with the mind as well as with the soul. Christ is yours, nothing can rob you of Him, of His life, of His example, of His influence, of His gospel, of His Church. For myself I can unhesitatingly say I cannot conceive anything whatever in all the possibility of critical and historical research that could weaken my hold of Christ, diminish my faith in Christ, chill my love of Christ. In the fearless words of a living divine, "We can listen to anything which historical criticism has to tell us of dates and authorship, of time and place. Our faith in Christ must determine what in the Bible is vital to its own vitality. It is the personal intimacy with God in Christ which alone is our concern. Belief can be only in Jesus Christ. To Him alone do we ever commit ourselves, surrender ourselves for ever and ever. Love is the distinctive prophecy of a future adherence; and our knowledge of Christ is the knowledge of love. What then can upset our trust in Him? What can disturb our knowledge of Him? What fear of change can the years bring on? Faith is moved by but one solitary passion—the hope

Canon Scott Holland.

of clinging closer and ever closer to the being of God." And the love which passeth knowledge is not our love to Him, but His love to us, Who is "the same yesterday, to-day, and for ever." *Hebrews xiii. 8.*

Lastly, its blessedness consists in the joy it brings with it; the joy which can never grow less; the joy which circumstances cannot imperil, nor change weaken, nor pain destroy; the joy of the harvest, when the wheat is gathered, and the waters crossed; the joy which Jesus tasted when His Passion was over; the joy which will be fulfilled, both for Him and for you, when you go to see His face. It is a wonderful thought, but not more wonderful than true, that we can add to the joy of Jesus. We can—the only thing to doubt about is, if we care to do so. We have given Him pain enough in the past; but it was as nothing for the love He bore us and the purpose He had to fulfil. When the high priest condemned Him, and the multitude cursed Him, and the priests taunted Him, and the soldiers crowned Him, a deep, ineffable, sustaining joy filled His soul—He was dying for the world; and the world one day would know it, and in part reward Him, by fulfilling His joy in a welcomed salvation. Let us all give Christ this joy—the joy of saving us, and teaching us, and comforting us, and using us, and sanctifying us, and crowning us; and He will requite us with much joy in return, which the world can neither give nor take away. To-day, once more He says to us, "Lovest thou me?" "My love for thee passeth all knowledge." Can we say in return—can all of us honestly, if humbly, say it: "Lord, Thou knowest all things, Thou knowest that I love Thee"?

John xxi. 17.

ITS RESULTS

This is the secret of every failure: we do not believe in the Holy Ghost."

BISHOP WESTCOTT.

VI

ITS RESULTS

The Church, which is his body."
EPHESIANS i. 22, 23.

AMONG the various evidences of a per- *Evidences* sonal Christ, Who lives, rules, and loves, none are more cogent than these three—the Bible, the Sacraments, and the Church. The Bible is the revelation of Christ's love, not only in the account it gives of its continuous manifestation, but also because it conveys to the devout heart the distinct impression of its sincerity and tenderness, as no other book in the world does. The Sacraments, both that which initiates the Divine life in man and that which edifies it, are the special channels and organs of His love. The Church is at once its result and witness. On the Church we will meditate now. May God help us to do so. For not only is it a solemn, yet blessed, responsibility for any teacher, sorrowfully conscious though he be of a supreme unworthiness, to try to write upon a subject so specially needing knowledge, and what Dean Church calls "calmness and breadth of equity"; it is also important to be guided, however imperfectly, and stirred, however feebly, about a theme which all through the æons in front will be the unfathomed mystery of our growing blessedness.

"Which is His body." Here is at once the fact and the outcome of the Incarnation, in which was planned from all eternity, and accomplished in the fulness of time, the Divine purpose for mankind.

The Church in her relation to Christ is sometimes spoken of as belonging to Christ, His most precious and tender possession; sometimes as very part of Him, an essential feature of His incarnate glory and endless life; sometimes also, in language of a loftiness that seems to rise above us into the clouds, as so identified with Him as to be, so to speak, Himself. In this same Epistle, for instance, we read of "His inheritance in the saints"—the saints whom, to borrow His own language, the Father had given Him out of the world;

Eph. i. 18.

described under a yet more tender and exquisite figure in the Revelation (and to be considered presently) as "the bride, the Lamb's wife." *Rev. xxi. 3.*

Here the Church is spoken of as His body— that living spiritual organism of which He is the head. Elsewhere we read of "the head, even Christ"; and again, "nourisheth and cherisheth" ("his own flesh") "even as the Lord the Church"; and once more in the First Epistle to the Corinthians, "Now ye are the body of Christ and members in particular." *Eph. iv. 15. Eph. v. 29. 1 Cor. xii. 27.* But in that same chapter the apostle in the eagerness of his burning desire to indicate and press the intimacy and oneness of the union between Christ and His people, is very bold, and hesitates not to describe them as one organic and substantial unity. "For as the body is one, and hath many members, and all the members of that one body, being many, are one body; so also is Christ." In other words, he will not suffer the Church to be described or even thought of as in any wise apart from her Lord. In the Divine idea, Christ is the Church, and the Church is Christ. *Vol. 2.*

The Church's function in the world is of a threefold character. It is a society, and a *The Church. function.*

witness, and a kingdom. Just as the body is a single totality of muscles and nerves, and flesh, and bones, and blood, in a complicated but wonderful harmony: so the first aspect in which the Church presents itself to the world is that of a fellowship of redeemed men, accepting one tribunal, obeying one authority, fired by one purpose, vitalised by one life; knowing and believing one eternal and unchangeable love, fearing but one baseness, the coming too far short of it.

Dean Church.

It has been finely said that "in all human society we see two ideas." In the first place, there is the actual work of life—what its members do, and what binds them one to another; the great and manifold order of civilised life. In the second place, all human society is the receptacle, nursery, and dwelling-place of ideas, judgments and governing principles of thought and action—and the doctrine of the Christian Church, which is one of the articles of the Apostles' Creed, means that religious ideas, like other ideas, if they are to have their perfect work, need a society to welcome them into reality and life, to exhibit them with whatever energy and force they possess, to preserve them from being pushed out or forgotten. "Books preserve ideas, but not their empire on minds." They must be contained and expressed "in the actual lives and speech of men." It was probably the social aspect of Christianity in the primitive time that made the Imperial power so jealous of its influence, and so suspicious of its progress. It is the social aspect and the common life of Christianity now that make it a power in the world.

Dean Church.

Being a society, it becomes a testimony. Men ask, What unites them? What inspires them? What is it they wish to do? What is it they fear to lose? Have they discovered what to others is a secret? Let them disclose their secret. If they have found a treasure which would make the whole race rich, let them share it with the race. The Church indeed has never, when true to herself, sought to hide her light under a bushel, or to keep back from king or slave what the Lord God has committed to her keeping. The fact of her existence is the crucial fact in the history of the universe. The grandeur of her hope is the only force that can save the race from despair.

But the society which is a witness is therefore a power; the most subtle, the most pervasive, the most irresistible, the most triumphant, the most permanent, the most elastic, ever seen on earth. It is so because its creed is a message of redemption, its end an assured victory, its secret the presence of God, its motive the enthusiasm of love. The Church is a kingdom of priests—in other words a Divine society of men who rule, worship, and serve. They rule first themselves, then others. They worship, and as they worship, God is seen, felt, received, and adored. They serve, because henceforth they live not unto themselves, but unto Him Who died for them and rose again, and Who whispers, not only to a chosen few, though indeed to them supremely and typically, but to every soul of man, baptised into His body:

Matt. iv. 19.

"Follow me, and I will make you fishers of men." Yes, the three great facts in the Church's life in the world are fellowship, testimony, and power; fellowship with men, springing out of fellowship with God; testi-

John iv. 42.

mony to men—"Now we believe, not because of thy saying, for we have heard Him ourselves"; power for men, for her work in the world is by the sword of the Spirit to conquer men for God, and to bring them as priceless spoils to the feet of Him Who was once nailed to the cross for their salvation, but Who now sits on the throne for their eternal life.

But the Church, for her outward manifestation and her continual progress, and her reasonable justification, and her sublime activities, needs organisation, polity, and methods. Each and all of these, as we may come to see presently, have been conferred on her by her Lord and Head in the counsel of an infinite love, at once the expression and the satisfaction of His personal relationship, and (what is perhaps not always so clearly seen) in the purpose of the discipline of a large and tolerant charity in the mutual association of her members.

Baptism makes us members of Christ and incorporates us into His body. In affirming this, which for most of us is happily beyond controversy, we impose no arbitrary limitations on the Divine compassion. We repudiate the cruel arrogance of denying to those who are outside the visible pale, through no fault of their own, either the favour of God or the possibility of living to His praise. But though we will not speculate as to what we do not know, we will, we must, urge what we do know, both as duty and privilege, safety and blessedness. By baptism we are admitted into the household of faith, and may claim all that the Divine adoption includes, and in being children we are brethren. "Herein is love, not that we loved God, but that He loved us, and sent His Son to be the propitiation for our sins. Beloved, if God so loved us, we ought also to love one another."

<small>*1 John iv. 10, 11.*</small>

The Church is the vast multitude of the baptised, and each baptised person is, by virtue and in reason of that baptism, the kinsman of his fellows. But how is this Church—so vast, so heterogeneous, so venerable, and yet so young—always changing, always moving, with her head in the clouds and her feet on the earth, to be ruled, administered, and served? Here we come to stand on difficult ground: difficult, because honeycombed with the controversies of centuries; difficult, because it can be usefully and profitably examined only with qualities which are at least rare, and with knowledge which is not at every man's disposal; difficult, because in the constitution of the human mind it is often found to be of much more consequence which aspect of truth is first presented to the mind for its critical and honest apprehension, than that which has most truth going with it; difficult, also, because prejudice so often obscures reason, and sentiment is preferred to history.

In this, as in all cognate subjects, there are several distinct courts of appeal. If we do not get much to help us from one, it is open to us to approach another; and if the result of our inquiry gives us ample satisfaction for our own position, we shall also be helped to appreciate the standing-ground of those who differ from us, and a generous respect for the liberty of brethren, who differ from us, will not be envenomed. We will add charity to decision, and respect where we may not concur.

Authority is the first court of appeal. "What saith the Scripture?" History is the second court of appeal. What has been the Church's practice and method from the earliest time till now? Where authority is silent, and history speaks with faltering voice, then, as Hooker would encourage us to do, we fall back gladly and fearlessly on reason. To buttress the conclusions of reason with the uncontroverted facts of a wide experience should complete a task which it is right to accept, cowardly to evade, impossible quite successfully to discharge.

Holy Scripture, which, with only half-a-dozen lines, might, had it so pleased God, have set the controversy at rest by preventing its very existence, is silent where we should have expected it to speak; omits what some would have given worlds to know. When St. Luke tells us that our Lord was not taken up into heaven until after He had, "through the Holy Ghost, given commandments unto the apostles whom he had chosen," the Evangelist is silent as to the details, though he assures us of the facts. "What commandments?" we ask, and no answer comes. In the very next verse we read that during the forty days' sojourn on earth between His resurrection and ascension, He was "speaking of the things pertaining to the kingdom of God." What those things were we can only conjecture, not

Acts i. 2.

Acts v. 3.

assert; and one man's conjecture is as good, and as useless, as another's. We read indeed that He promised to be with His disciples alway unto the end of the world. But this grand promise will hardly serve as the sufficient basis of a definite and authoritative organisation. St. Paul has written of Him that "He gave some apostles, and some prophets, and some evangelists, and some pastors and teachers, for the perfecting of the saints, for the work of the ministry, for the edifying of the body of Christ." But we discover here, not so much a code of government as an act of benevolence; and some of these functions were evidently for the circumstances of the time, and have passed with the inevitable changes. It almost seems as if the Lord had of purpose intended His Church to go to Him from time to time for the wisdom and guidance she needed, as she needed it; and not to cramp her liberty, and forestall her necessities, and weaken her responsibility by prematurely ordaining a stereotyped and universal organisation, instead of leaving her to observe His providence and accept His guidance as the multiplying years might indicate. The Lord

Eph. iv. 11, 12.

honours us, tests us, and trusts us in leaving us very free. Nevertheless, history presently shows us, with a helpful distinctness, what we may presume the Lord's mind to have been about His Church, by the way in which, with a universal and almost instinctive consent, she adopted and authorised and transmitted that form of government which we recognise and accept in our Church of England. As the Prayer Book asserts, "It is evident unto all men reading diligently the Holy Scriptures and ancient authors, that from the apostles' time there have been these orders of ministers in Christ's Church—Bishops, Priests, and Deacons." It is true, of course, that for the first few years of the second century there is a silence and a twilight about the matter. But the most exact and learned scholars of this our critical and erudite time are absolutely clear that about the middle of that century, bishops, who during the lifetime of the apostles may have been identified with presbyters, came by common consent, and, we may add, by the guidance of the Holy Ghost and the will of the Church's Head, to inherit the place of authority once held by the apostles.

Preface to the Ordinal.

To them was given the great duty of ordaining and confirming, of ruling and administering; inheritors of the magnificent promise of the Lord's uninterrupted presence, they presumably ministered His grace and wielded His power.

What history declares, reason weighs and interprets. She will be careful indeed not to conclude more than what the facts justify. The guarded and precise language of the Prayer Book about the three orders, in confining itself to a firm declaration of the fact, without forcing any arbitrary inference from it, should be a lesson to those who, in their reasonable eagerness to make their own position as strong as possible, claim for it more than the evidence will really afford. But if for all the centuries quite down to the period of the Reformation, this has been, all over the world, the one accepted and authorised organisation for the body of Christ, and if it be the case that men neither apparently wished, nor actively sought, nor in any sense succeeded in creating any other, there is at least good cause for inferring that it was the gift of God, as well as the purpose of God, for His redeemed people; and experience, while it is a two-edged sword for a bitter and exclusive arrogance, on whichever side it shows itself, comes in to assist and corroborate reason. If in this enlightened, and enquiring, and critical, and energetic time, the Anglican Church, with her complete and apostolic discipline and order, so far from having exhausted her strength and lost her vitality, seems endowed with a fresh youth, and is stretching out her open arms of welcome and blessing to the uttermost ends of the earth, we hail the lesson of experience that God is still with her, her refuge and strength, her sun and shield. It is true also—and who will deny the fact, or grudge it, with a sour and unchristian envy?—that religious bodies outside us, with organisation different to ours, and worship dissociated from ours, manifest a zeal, and a fellowship, and a spirit of sacrifice, and a burning love of morality, which could hardly be theirs if Christ the Lord did not send down His Holy Spirit upon them; would even be impossible for them if the Eternal Father did not behold and bless them in the Son of His love, and give them, in answer to their motives, their efforts, their prayers, the benediction of an abundant fruitfulness.

The scope of the Church's duty is fourfold: to protect morals, to maintain and propagate the faith, to be the handmaid and voice of the Lord, to be the revelation of God. What the Jews were to the heathen before Christ, the Church is to be to the world until Christ comes back—the stern, unflinching champion of purity and temperance, of honesty and justice, of forbearance and love, of patience and self-sacrifice. If the Church does not exist to make the world better, what is she good for? Goodness is the Divine purpose in everything. The Lord's sentence to His disciples in the Sermon on the Mount is His message to the Church of all times: "Ye are the salt of the earth; ye are the light of the world." This may from time to time involve painful isolation, inevitable misconstruction, chilling the regard of friends, exasperating the enmity of foes. She will sometimes have to be eccentric and obstinate; to keep her eyes open when worldly wisdom would close them; to open her lips for plain speaking and rebuke when a sleek prudence would be silent. Opportunities of influence will seem to be lost through excessive frankness, and friends be

The scope of her duty.

Matt. v. 13, 14.

bitterly alienated because it was impossible to please God without displeasing man; but virtue must be maintained, and a lofty standard of goodness held up, and marriage girt about with the Divine restraints, and the words and looks of licence hushed and shamed by indignant innocence. "If the salt have lost his savour, wherewith shall it be seasoned?" If the Church is cowed, or dumb, or bribed, or tempted into connivance with evil, Christ is once more betrayed into the power of His enemies, and consecrated hands will nail Him to a second cross.

Luke xiv. 34.

The Church is to be a keeper of Holy Writ —eagerly to contend for the faith once delivered to the saints; at home, to hold fast at any cost the blessed privilege of teaching the young in the faith of Christ at school, to spread abroad the glad tidings of the Gospel to the uttermost ends of the earth; to be the messenger of the Divine pity to those everywhere who are fast "bound in misery and iron." Of course, she must distinguish the things that differ, and be sure it is Scripture she is defending, before she draws her sword to defend it. "If the foundations be destroyed, what shall

Psalm xi. 3.

the righteous do?" She must hold in an inflexible and tenacious grasp every single article of the Catholic faith necessary to salvation; but she must not encumber the vessel's deck with cargo that does not properly belong to it; she must accurately and wisely distinguish between doctrines that constitute the faith, and opinions that may plausibly be deduced from it.

She is to be the handmaid and voice of her Lord, declaring Him, representing Him, imitating Him, taking Him to the prison cell and the groaning battlefield, to the house of mourning and the place of festal gladness; to the well-filled board of the rich and to the humble cottage of the poor; to the senate with her august authority, to the pulpit with her inspired message. When the Church helps men to understand, and trust, and accept, and follow Christ, she is true to herself and to Him. When the thought, and beauty, and presence, and glory of Christ die out of the world's imagination like the colours of the sky when the sun has dropped behind the mountains, it is because the Church slumbers and sleeps.

Yes, she is to be the revelation of God; to be filled with God, to take the impression of Him where she goes, to bequeath the impression of Him where she leaves; not to terrify, but to elevate; not to rebuke, but to win; and this without meaning it or knowing it, without thought of self-righteousness or taint of egotism. Of course, it means much, appallingly much; and it is a height not reached in a day, a sort of Alpine ridge, which has the first touch of the rising sun, and the last of the setting; which commands the wide expanse of humanity at its feet, the humanity it has been redeemed and called to serve, and which it should behold only to love, pity, and heal.

It is possible enough to conceive of Christ's love for the Church as a whole. We think of the glorious company of the apostles, of the goodly fellowship of the prophets, of the noble army of martyrs, of the spirits and souls of the righteous, of the great flock in all parts of the world who set forth the eternal praise of His holy name. The great multitude which no man can number may well, indeed, be the object of His love. But just as the astronomer, who with his glass sweeps the starry plains of heaven and detects millions of worlds which he can neither weigh, nor count, nor measure—only he knows them to be there—feels baffled by the mystery that He Who filled the sky with the splendour of His creative wisdom can stoop to lavish skill on a flower of the field, with beauty passing all the glory of Solomon; we each ask—how can He think of me, care for me, enter into my needs, waste any of His love on a creature so feeble and so vile? It is a thought dwelt upon already, perhaps can hardly *P. 112.* be dwelt upon too much or too often. And the only answer is this: He is God, and He has made me in His image; and if I thirst and long for His love it is His own doing. Perhaps no one can really possess the fruition of the love of God without often feeling utterly unworthy of it, unspeakably amazed by it. It was when the Lord had at His heart to call Simon Peter to the apostleship that he said: "Depart from me, for I am a sinful man, O *Luke v. 8.* Lord." But the sense of our unworthiness is the best possible proof that He is near us, and gazing on us with unspeakable tenderness. It is when the bush burns that God would speak. What created thing is worthy of God's love?

But what created thing should not believe, and welcome, and receive it?

C. Rossetti
> "Yea, I have sought thee; yea, I have found thee;
> Yea, I have thirsted for thee;
> Years long ago with love's bands I bound thee;
> Now the everlasting arms surround thee;
> Through death's darkness I look and see,
> And clasp thee to me."

The thought of Christ's love to His Church, and to each living member of it, has its inspiring as well as its consoling side. It admonishes us of duty, as well as assures us of blessing. If we find it wonderful that God should love us, we sometimes feel it strange and hard to love one another; and in this case not so much from active hostility or unsuitable behaviour, but merely because our brother wounds our self-love on its most sensitive side, in differing from our cherished opinions, or even opposing our well-meant schemes. We feel wronged by it, and, without any attempt to do him justice, we resent it as a personal wrong. Yet he, too, may claim to be taught of God, and feel to be used by Him, and expect to be welcomed by Him when he passes into His presence to enjoy Him for ever; and who shall dare to say that in so hoping he presumes more than we?

Surely this wonderful thought of Christ's love to us should teach and help us to love one another. Love, of course, is distinct from friendship. Every man is my neighbour, only a few can be my friends. But to have a lofty, generous, frank, and trusty regard to those brethren who, if they cannot walk with us, are only on the other side of the road that leads to the Celestial City; who use our Bible, accept our creeds, serve our Lord, seek our home—
—this should not be too hard for us, if we remember that those who are dear to Christ should be esteemed by us. There need be no mawkish insincerity, no affectation of a unity that does not really exist; simply the goodwill and trustful respect for those whom the laws of the human mind keep apart on this side eternity, but who, in the full light of the Lamb, shall meet and greet as friends.

This love of Christ—do we all feel to know and possess it for ourselves? And have we as much of it as we please, and would we learn the secret of its deepest and most satisfying joy?

There are two conditions for this. One, *Conditions.* faith; the other, obedience. The love of God is shed abroad in our hearts by the Holy Ghost which is given unto us. Believe me, we cannot make ourselves love God; neither can we stir, or deepen, or augment our sense of His love to us by any violent effort of our own. We must just take it on trust that He loves us, because He says so, and because our lives are one continuous proof of it, and wait to receive His blessing as it pleases Him to let it come. We want to cultivate the receptive faculty in our souls—more to ask, more to seek, more to knock, more to hunger and thirst, more to hope, and wait, and praise. He is not always telling us how He loves us, nor stimulating our pulses to feel it. He knows that we must not be fed with cordials; that faith, not sight, is the secret of our spiritual manhood. But, when we really need it, He will come and say: "Fear not, I will help thee." As Peter sank beneath the black waters, the Lord's hand snatched him, and His voice encouraged him. He, too, sometimes asks of us that we should show and express our love to Him, Who thrice asked of the apostle who had denied Him, "Lovest thou me more than these?"

Isaiah xli. 13.

John xxi. 15.

We must also remember that, as sorrow is the discipline for tasting His love, indulged sin of any kind is fatal to our growing perception of it. Christ's law here, as everywhere else, is self-acting. The heart that is filled with the world's possessions, and activities, and ambitions, and society, has not eyesight, nor hearing for the still small voice of the waiting Saviour; and any taint of self-indulgence, or pride, or resentment, sends Him sorrowful away. The Lord who loves us longs for our holiness, and we must not resent the means He takes for accomplishing in us the end of His Incarnate life. He " loved the Church, and gave Himself for it, that He might sanctify and cleanse it by the washing of water and by the Word, that He might present it to Himself a glorious Church, not having spot, or wrinkle, or any such thing; but that it should be holy and without blemish." *Eph. v. 25, 26, 27.*

Lastly, as the bodily strength decays, and friend after friend passes behind the veil that separates us from the invisible world, and the joy of noble activities becomes less and less possible, and we soon expect to turn the corner in the road, where the mountains of the

Delectable Land rise up against the sky, and Jordan rolls at our feet—what shall be our supreme hope, the summit of all possible felicity, the goal of the weary pilgrimage of tedious years, but the vision, the welcome, the seen and tasted love of Him Who has waited to be gracious ever since He first called us to His service, and Who has longed and wished for us far more than we for Him? Oh, what it will be to enter into the joy of the Lord!—the joy of sin forgiven, of death conquered, of friends reunited, of tears wiped away; but, most of all—most of all—the joy of the love of eternal God filling every pulse of the cleansed and sinless soul with unspeakable sweetness, as the fulness of the rising tide fills every nook and cavity on the shore.

Then we shall understand what perplexes us now; then we shall welcome what pains us now; then we shall lament what contents us now; then we shall surrender what we half wish to detain now. When we see Him as He is (we shall not be strange to Him, He knows all about us already), we shall begin to love Him as He deserves.

IN DEATH

> *"All the preaching since Adam has not made death other than death."*
>
> PREBENDARY EYTON.

VII

IN DEATH

"When thou passest through the waters I will be with thee, and through the rivers, they shall not overflow thee."—ISAIAH xlii. 3.

WHEN Bunyan in his immortal allegory draws a picture, full of pathos and dignity, of Christian and Hopeful wading through the deep waters to the Celestial City in front, he puts these words into Hopeful's lips, to soothe the tremors of his friend. Preachers and poets, too, when impressing on mortal ears the struggles, and yet the triumphs, of the last scene in our mortal history, hasten to borrow an illustration which time cannot make common nor experience decry as unreal. That infinite and ineffable love on which we have tried to meditate, so lofty and yet so tender, so awful and yet so sweet, is never more pitiful, more exquisite, more all-sufficing, more exactly expressed than in these words at that supreme hour.

Death sometimes tedious.

What we call death, moreover, for not a few souls -ours it may be among them—is by no means to be confined to the exact moment of physical dissolution. Some men take long to die. For many, when he comes to shake his insolent spear in their face, the Amalekite's answer is their answer: "The bitterness of death is passed." The one event that comes alike to all not unfrequently projects its gloomy shadows upon even distant years, slowly and remorsefully endured in a protracted autumn. When the apostle said, "I die daily," he may, of course, have referred to the "deaths oft" in which he carried his life in his hand, whether from the paroxysms of popular fury or the sudden storms of the Midland Sea. There are still true saints of God, lovely and blessed in their lives, who have bands in their death of which children of this world know nothing. At eventime it is not light with them; the sacrifice is being salted with fire up to the moment that the summons comes. They are not finishing their course with joy; they know

1 Sam. xv. 32.

1 Cor. xv. 31.
2 Cor. xi. 23.

nothing of "the joy of harvest." Yet if friends *Isaiah ix.* lament, and the Church is disappointed, and the world wonders, the Saviour understands and overrules all. He, at least, has no frown or reproof for the heart which is full of misery only because His face is clouded; nay He presses us more closely to Him, and loves us for it, if possible, better than before. He knoweth whereof he made us; He sees that we are true, and that the one thing we care for is His presence.

It may be helpful (and the subject is not too *Reasons for this.* frequently treated) to examine at least some of the causes which help to explain why a Christian's last years are sometimes shadowed, if not gloomy; which, while they make the waters all round him like the swellings of Jordan, at the very moment when he needs steadiness most, all but carry him off his feet.

And perhaps the first in order, if not in *Imperfect penitence.* importance, is the not uncommon fact of an imperfect and shallow penitence which, while in a measure comprehending the sinfulness of sin, and the awful majesty of the Divine holiness, has yet to learn more thoroughly to hate, to loathe, to fear, to crucify it; to apprehend its malignity as compassing the death of Christ, to fathom its deceitfulness in hiding us so subtly from ourselves. Not always is there an adequate appreciation of the vital distinction between repentance and penitence. Repentance is the first glance at the glory of a righteous God, grieved and angry at our sin. Penitence is the continuous vision of His holy face, in sympathy with His abhorrence of evil, and accepting His methods of overcoming it. Repentance is the quick and sudden spasm of a heart into which God's arrow has penetrated, eagerly, impatiently, asking for the wound to be healed. Penitence is the lifelong and growing knowledge of the inner corruption of nature, and of the awful "depths of Satan" which constantly stirred it into life. Repentance is the awakening of the consciousness of sin; and penitence is the ever-deepening abhorrence of its sinfulness. Repentance resolves on amendment. Penitence confirms and perfects it in walking humbly with God. Repentance may be quite sincere; it may be acceptable so far as it goes, and a genuine work of the Spirit of God, and even fruitful in an entire and permanent conversion, while through such causes as

Rev. ii. 24

scanty leisure, incessant pressure, shallow and emotional teaching, and a lack of sustained meditation, it remains altogether on the surface of the soul, and has never penetrated into its inner chambers, nor seen God face to face to praise Him in His holiness.

But these are lessons that must be learned some time or other through a discipline which cannot be quite dispensed with on this side of Paradise. If it does not come soon, it comes late. It is not sufficient to say of it that the regimen is different for different souls, that in this common sinfulness all share, and so in this deep penitence all need severally to partake. It often comes in the closing years of life, when the door is shut upon the noise of the world, and there is leisure, such as there never was before, for self-discovery, for a retrospect of the past, for communion with God, for that looking on into the invisible world with thoughts of which, when very real and solemn, we cannot say much even to the dearest on earth. Then it is that we make discoveries of ourselves we never guessed before. Sins of our youth come back to us like lurid ghosts from a valley of tombs. God is felt to be not only our Father, but our Holy Father; with Job we abhor ourselves and repent in dust and ashes. One channel through which the sense of sin is deepened in us, is sometimes found (as David found it) in the persons of our children, when they are growing up, or even quite grown up; when the barriers and limitations of childhood have been one by one removed, when full opportunity of manifesting what they are is given, and the result too often —as we think, unfortunately—turns out a displeasing reproduction of ourselves. Do they somewhat fret at authority? So perhaps did we. Do they find home dull, duty tedious, the conventions of life insupportable, and their parents' society to have no attractiveness in it? So perhaps was it with some of us. Have they even grievously sinned, and we have reproached sharply, vehemently, and with a sense of injustice? Does not a whisper come, "Do you remember doing yourself exactly the same thing fifty years ago?" Are they infirm of purpose, and have we never been chargeable with inconstancy? Does it seem ungrateful or undutiful in them that our company is not always pleasant, and that they chiefly come to us when they want us to do something for them? Well, ingratitude of this sort has the seed of heredity in it. We know in our secret hearts that, if our parents could come back from the dead, we should try to love them with more tenderness and minister to them with more vigilance, and dutifully cherish their society, and joyfully anticipate their wishes, more than ever we did when they were here on earth.

Further, these children of ours, who we think owe so much to us, but do not always see what they owe, still less care to pay it, minister to us without their knowing it, a message with which we could not dispense, and a discipline which is to deepen in us, as nothing else can, a sad thirst for holiness. If the duty is still the same for us occasionally to forbid, to restrain, to reprove, let us do it with a moderated displeasure, and with the equipoise of a secret self-reproach. Just because we love them so much, their faults and shortcomings distress us. But they are God's as well as ours, and in their own time and generation the experience we are suffering will duly and inevitably pass on to them. The recollection of past neglect, never, it may be, adequately mourned over or hated, cannot but bring with it a clouded and dark sky, when outward activities can be no foil to the reproaches of conscience. It is not as the singing of birds when the spring is coming, nor the lowing of the patient oxen taking home the harvest sheaves. We mourn for our children, we are shamed for our God, we are ill at peace with ourselves. The past cannot be lived again. It is too late. Men and women can never be children again. The opportunity is over, and the thought of our loss steeps us in sadness.

Another circumstance often goes to make the gathering waters of our last hours chilly and deep. Results are coming in. Mistakes are unfolding themselves, disappointments bite us with a sharp and jagged tooth. Opportunities which, now that they are gone, we appreciate at their value, we have missed, and who can bring them back? Let no one say all this is morbid, and foolish, and useless, and the feeble querulousness of a mind slipping off its balance. Adjectives cannot change facts; and if there was no sense of failure, and no pain of disappointment, none of us could learn anything;

and the world would never progress. These experiences, moreover, cover all the surface of our life in matters of secular business, such as investments and savings; in questions of trust and patronage, about those whom we thought to possess the needful qualifications for offices of duty, and who have turned out to have possessed none of them. We discover and lament mistakes which not only affect our credit for sagacity and our instinct of even a tolerable prudence, but which injure and impair others as well as ourselves, and may go on injuring and impairing them long after we are gone and forgotten. Confidence misplaced, trusts placed in unworthy hands, not without inquiry, but it may be with insufficient inquiry; occasions for counsel or kindness, the preciousness, the beautifulness of which cannot be put into words, have been slightingly glanced at, or helplessly deferred, and now they are for ever gone.

He is a wise man (is wise the right word?) who can always acquit himself of errors. He is a fortunate man who, coming in his life's journey to a parting of the ways, and being compelled suddenly, and almost blindly, to take one of them, never happens to take the one which, as it turns out, he ought not to have taken, and so laments it till he dies. He is a supremely prudent man who never accepts any one's warmest assurances about any one else, and is never misled, because he never has the generosity for trusting.

These ghosts of the past (who does not know them in one shape or another?) come to us at all moments and in all places. The happiness of other homes seems to taunt us with our own disorder. The diligent and prosperous sons of other fathers fill us with covetous hope, or stir us to an agony of prayer. Something in the street as we pass recalls them to us; and there are some troubles which act like a seton in the heart. At night before we sleep, in the dark morning long before it is time to rise, they banish repose or make it impossible. They come, and they go, and they return, for they are always with us. It needs manhood to bear them without sharing them with others; it needs faith, almost a sublime faith, to be well assured that all things, and even these among the all, are permitted, and can be overruled for blessing.

Further than this there is, with some of us
—who shall say there ought not to be with all?
—a grievous sense of shortcoming and imperfection in duty, a languor and shallowness in
the spiritual apprehension of God, a profound
feeling of shamefulness at the undevoutness
and undisciplinedness of our souls. Any one
who has read the " Adieux " of Adolphe Monod
(a transparent, saintly, and healthy soul, if ever
there was one), will easily comprehend what I
mean. All wisdom and spiritual understanding
is not only a privilege but a duty. How much
hangs on it, how much comes out of it? But
it will not come by intuition, though occasionally a deep truth will suddenly flash on us like
a meteor in the sky, to light up all the other
truths already centred there, and to reconcile
them into a beautiful and consistent harmony.
To be Christlike—is not that the end, the aim,
the hope, the reward of all? It is partly to be
ours now, completely to be ours hereafter.
Now and here "beholding as in a glass the
glory of the Lord, we are changed into the
same image from glory to glory, even as by the
Spirit of the Lord." Presently, the beautiful
vision will be the completed transfiguration:

2 Cor. iii. 18.

1 John iii. 2. "We shall be like Him, for we shall see Him as He is."

Who, then, can wonder, or even justly complain, if the true and self-searching soul, travelling over its past journey, weighing the greatness of its stewardship, counting up the list of its failures and mistakes, contrasting its own meagre and impoverished goodness with the lofty ideal of the majestic holiness of the King in His beauty, Whom it feels to be on the way, soon, it may be to-morrow, to see, is sometimes abashed and disconsolate, and dumb; if it forgets its anthem of praise in its psalm of penitence; if for a little moment it fails to remember the apostle's conviction that what things were gain to him, those he counted loss for Christ: that his aim and hope, like our own hope, was to be found in Him, not having his own righteousness, but the righteousness of God—by faith; the only way of peace, the one secret of joy.

Thus when we apprehend and hold fast, the clouds disperse, and there is the clear shining after the rain.

Here let me interpolate, for the better understanding of what has gone before, and will follow, some reflections which should act as guiding principles in a shadowed topic which cannot well have too much light on it.

Death is still the inherited penalty of sin, and can never be anything else. Its sting may be blunted, and its empire broken: it is no longer the end of life, it is but an incident in it. But Christ died, not to save us from dying, but to show us how to die; and He rose again that He might be *Lord* both of the dead and living. If no longer death can be called with perfect accuracy the King of Terrors— for his power has been broken and to the Christian death is but falling asleep—only a few elect souls like Francis d'Assisi in the Middle Ages, and Bernard Gilpin in ours, ravished with the joy of the hope of what comes after it, can welcome it, even bless it when it comes. At the best we meet it calmly, we obey it dutifully, we accept it trustfully; but there is still the taint of a curse upon it, and we shall be glad when it is behind us.

To escape all tremor and sadness, and even anguish in death, might mean to miss an untold and vast blessing, which would make all the difference both to our last years on earth and to our entrance as well as our place in Paradise; nay, it might be to forfeit all that beautiful, though often sharp, discipline which He who loves us with a holy love cannot spare us, just because He loves us, and which we should not wish Him to spare us, if we knew all that it intends. "This light affliction, which is but for a moment, worketh for us a far more exceeding and eternal weight of glory." "Light," that is, when contrasted with what is to come out of it, though its "lightness" now might seem a burden heavier than we can possibly bear. Some of God's people seem always to be in the furnace; and we wonder at it while we mourn for them. There are always two good reasons for it: one, the truth of which is plain enough to them; the other, the blessedness of which is plain enough to the Church. The Christian himself, one day taken out of the fire and the next day put back into it and kept there, if now and then in his distress he asks himself, "What have I done that I endure such affliction?" soon recovers himself, and on his knees pours out his complaint to God. "I need it all, I deserve

2 Cor. iv. 17.

it all; only show me Thy love that I may be helped to bear it; and give me Thy grace, that in the end it may all redound to Thy glory." The Church stands by and watches, and suffers and prays; and the tried disciple is felt to be bearing about in his body the dying of the Lord Jesus, that the life also of Jesus may be made manifest in his mortal flesh.

For to some, if not all, death is the last occasion, with the living at least, and on this side of the invisible world, of glorifying God; of manifesting, not only by activity, but by patience; not only by going about, but by lying still; not only by speaking, but by silence; not only by emotion, but by faith, what the love of Christ is to those who can trust Him with everything, and how even the travail of death is but a fuller birth of the soul into the light and glory of God. There are circumstances when to leave children and duty behind us means agony. To suffer is not sinful. A stolid passionless torpor is not at all the temper that magnifies Christ or edifies men. But keenly and largely to value all we are leaving and yet to manifest as well as to say, that " to depart and be with Christ" "is far better," means

Phil. i. 23.

a testimony that may bring souls to Christ long after we have gone to Him; preaches a sermon that shall go on repeating its message when we are singing the new song with the angels of God.

But now we approach the central, vital essence of the subject before us, how the love of Christ is our solid and abiding consolation for a moment when our strength fails us and for an event which we have to meet alone. His love is the love of One Who has Himself once gone through it all, and Who can never forget what it meant for Him. His love is the love of One Who, because He knows, understands; Who, because He understands, is filled with sympathy. His love is the love of One Who said of Himself, "Greater love hath no man than this, that he lay down his life for his friends." What His sacrifice implies, contains, and declares is best expressed in the apostle's sentence, "He hath made Him sin for us that we might be made the righteousness of God in Him." It is the love of One Who went out to do battle for us, and has conquered in it, and Whose victory is as much our victory as if we had won it all by ourselves. It is the

John xv. 13.

2 Cor. v. 21

love of One Who, by the inspiration of His Spirit, has directed St. Paul to compare His love to the Church with the love of a husband to his wife; love in the marvellous expression of an exquisite tenderness, abundantly manifested when there is a real need for it; when the heart is breaking, and the life is ebbing, and the Tempter is at hand to whisper desertion and abandonment, and the friends at our side can only watch and pray and weep. Christ has tasted death, tasted it for every man, and in anticipation of it His human soul trembled and quivered with suffering, though when the moment of departure came He fell asleep in peace. He knows all about it, and perhaps the truest key to the meaning of the agony in the garden and of the sense of desertion on the cross, is that, suffering as the representative of a guilty race, He consented, nay, in a sense, was constrained, to feel what that guiltiness merited in the eyes of a holy God; and loving God as only the Son of His love could love Him, understanding God as only His divine nature could help Him to understand, and yet sorrowing for man as only His kinsman and representative could sorrow, He felt the burden, loathed the shame, abhorred the guilt; and so when death, which at once represents the Father's holiness and the world's penalty, came nearer, for a brief moment the cross seemed insupportable. "Who in the days of His flesh, and when he had offered up prayers and supplications with strong crying and tears unto Him that was able to save Him from death, and was heard in that he feared."

Heb. v. 7.

No one but Christ knows what it really means to die. No one but Christ can assure us that not a hair of our head shall perish, as we pass on our solitary journey into the invisible world. We cannot tell all that this will mean to us when we want it, for He does not comfort till the time of comforting arrives. But if we are sure of Him and of our interest in Him, we may be as sure as of our own existence that His personal experience will enable Him to feel, to meet, to soothe the secret and individual tremors of each separate soul as it makes its flight to Him; that "He is able also to save to the uttermost" all that come unto God by Him. For, be it observed further, His power of consoling and the real value of His love depend, essentially depend, on the

Heb. vii. 25.

mystery of His person, and on the completeness of His sacrifice. Here the dogma of the Catholic Faith is an impregnable rock on which our faith must be builded. It is not only that we know in Whom we have believed, but also that we know what we believe about Him, that our Friend is also our Saviour, and that His love as man is also combined with His love as God. Son of Man—here is the capacity for His passion; Son of God—here is the infinite merit of it. He has died and risen again. He has offered a sacrifice which was at once voluntary, flawless, and complete. His sacrifice does not only mean His death, it also includes His life: the life which fulfilled all righteousness, with the death which consummated it. Substitute, representative, victim, atonement—these are but the inadequate expressions of various aspects of a vast and many-sided mystery, which in its completeness means that Christ is our peace, for life and death, for judgment and eternity. He is everything to us or He is nothing to us: there is no middle term between these two positions. " Declared to be the Son of God with power, by the resurrection from the dead " He is made *Romans i. 4.*

Heb. v. 9. "the author of eternal salvation to all them that obey Him."

If all this is true, let us use it resolutely and continually when the time comes for using it, and say again and again to ourselves, are there blesseder words that dying lips can utter?

> "Rock of ages, cleft for me,
> Let me hide myself in Thee;
> Let the water and the blood
> From Thy riven side which flowed
> Be of sin the double cure,
> Cleanse me from its guilt and power."

Dogma is meant to be a help to the thinking part of man, and it is doubtful if we use it as it is meant to be used. It is truth that makes us free, free from the bondage of fear and the foundering of unbelief. The truth is that *John iii. 16.* "God so loved the world that He gave His only begotten Son that whosoever believeth in Him should not perish but have everlasting life."

Yes; and after death He is conqueror too. *Rev. i. 18.* "I am He that liveth and was dead, and have the keys of death and Hades."

Death is conquered, for Jesus has conquered it, and we shall conquer it in Him. Between the vision of Him in Paradise and the putting on of our resurrection glory, when He comes in the clouds to judge the world, there will be an interval. To speculate on the length of this interval is to forget that in the world to come we shall cease to be subject to the limitations of time; to meditate on our employment of it is indeed a reasonable and even helpful study, if we are careful not to be wise above that which is written, and not to intrude into things which are not seen—" vainly puffed Col. ii. 18. up with "our" fleshy mind." We are to " seek Col. iii. 1. those things which are above, where Christ sitteth on the right hand of God." Surely, however, thinking is seeking of the best kind, and the things which are above may well be thought to include the entire administration of the world of spirits.

"To be with Christ" describes the safety and blessedness of the companionship; to fall asleep in Christ implies the tranquillity and sanctity of the repose.

Outside these sentences all is in shadow. Each one can imagine for himself. No one must impose on his neighbour what within them may safely be held.

But the truth of truths, the promise of promises, is this, "whether we live therefore or die" we are the Lord's—His personal possession, the spoils of His bitter cross, the product of His pruning and training, the final result of all He has done for us, and with us, and by us, while we were in this world. We are safe in the everlasting arms, from which neither man nor angel shall pluck us. He watches us as we depart, His angels convey us into His beatific presence, our dust in the grave has a certain preciousness for Him; for are not these mortal bodies temples of the Holy Ghost? How much more the spirits, made in His Divine image, with which we have loved and worshipped and served Him till our ministry was done?

To some persons the fear of death, in spite of what they actually know of Christ and of the joy of His full salvation, is a very real bondage, and a very humiliating terror. It is always with them, dogging their path, overshadowing their life, poisoning their innocent joy, taking out of their worship and duty all flavour and strength. It is but little to the purpose to excuse it by a physical nervous-

Roma xiv. 8.

ness, bound up with a keen vitality, or a constitutional liability to disease. That may explain, but it cannot console. Of course it can be accounted for, though not even then to be treated with indulgence, when constant illness, or a sudden and unaccountable attack of formidable disease, has invested life with an unavoidable sense of insecurity, and made us live from hand to mouth, as if a crevasse were yawning at our feet.

This is, however, quite a different thing from that fear of death which paralyses if it does not dishonour; though here, too, the sense of Christ's love, and of His perpetual overruling providence, stills the spirit into a great calm. Surely, the more excellent way is that of taking it, with all its exhausting, harassing painfulness, to the very feet of the Lord, and leaving it with Him. Surely this is just one of those instances to which St. Peter referred when he wrote the words—words with an infinite scope and meaning: "Casting all your care upon Him, for He careth for you." Nothing can give the soul, anticipating its awful future, the peace and hope it desires, *1 Pet. v. 7.*

but faith. This faith is at once deepened and fed by prayer.

Another way of using Christ's love as a remedy and support when we pass through the waters, is to try to get beyond death, and then in imagination look back as from behind it. Let us take measure now, in some degree, as we shall take measure then, of the worst that it can possibly mean for those who are the beloved of the Lord. Its worst will not seem very bad, nor its conflict doubtful, nor its struggles long, nor its solitariness real. Of course there are all varieties in the places, and modes, and circumstances of the last scene of trial. The cup is mixed to suit the soul that drinks it, and for no two persons is it ever quite the same. But it is soon over, and when it is over we shall wonder that we dreaded it so much and thought of it so fearfully.

There are two extremes in men's views of death. One is to make too little of it; the other is to make too much of it. Let us do neither. If Christ has abolished death, and if there is a permanent meaning in His words to Martha, "Whoever liveth and believeth in me shall never die," there is something unchristian

John xi. 26.

and even degrading in treating or anticipating it,
as if we lived and died amid the shadows of a
pagan world. Yet, when we think from what
it separates us, and to what it introduces us,
what it will mean for the human soul in its
nakedness and feebleness to appear before
God, and what a tremendous thing it will be
presently to receive at the Judge's hand all the
things that we have done in the body here,
there is something almost appalling in the
ever-nearing approach of the Divine messenger. Even St. Paul, who sings his majestic
pæan over it, does not scruple to speak of it
as an enemy to be overcome; but he adds for
our consolation that it is the last enemy we
shall ever have to meet, and that we shall not
meet it alone. The holiness of God, the inevitableness of judgment, the end of opportunity,
are tremendous realities. But against them all
we have this triumphant challenge: "If God
be for us, who can be against us?"

Rom. viii. 31.

After all, the secret of secrets is to sanctify
the Lord God in our hearts, and to look out
from the pavilion of His indwelling presence
on the gathering waterfloods and the boister-
ous river. He rewards faith with perfect

peace, and to the soul that looks to Him He tenderly whispers, "I am thy salvation." Nay, even if with Simon Peter, as we walk on the water to go to Him, for a moment the noise of the wind, and the blackness of the night, and the chill of the waters startle us, and we begin to sink, only let us remember to say, "Lord, save me!" and His right hand shall grasp us as it grasped the apostle, and we shall be with Him in the ship and reach the land.

Rev. John Keble.

"When the shore is won at last,
Who will count the billows past?"

IN JUDGMENT

"*The lips of the judge need not open to pronounce any sentence. He but lifts off each constraining law, each limiting infirmity, each instrument of education, and the result speaks for itself. Each soul by its own inner tendency seeks its own place.*"

PREBENDARY EYTON.

VIII

IN JUDGMENT

"*Herein is our love made perfect, that we may have boldness in the day of judgment; because as He is, so are we in this world.*"

1 JOHN iv. 17.

MORE exactly rendered, the opening sentence will run, " In this hath love been perfected between us "—*i.e.*, in the fellowship of God with man, and of man with God. In other words, this is the sublime triumph which love, believed, absorbed, and returned, shall achieve in its complete manifestation at the day of judgment. In that day, of which the apostle here and elsewhere has taught us so much and with such detail, and which will manifest to the human conscience the consummation of its moral history, the revelation of its self-made condition, and its supreme destiny, in the inevitable righteousness of God, he who has yielded to love, walked in it, brought others into it, increasingly learned its infinite and ineffable blessedness, shall, without the effrontery of hardness, or the callousness of an ignorance born of sin, but in a perfect peace, the very gift of God Himself, meet and behold the Judge without anguish or terror. This is a great mystery, but the apostle's statement is as clear as words can make it, and we cannot doubt what he means. Nevertheless, we shall do well to look into it, for who is there whom it does not concern? There are always some who say to themselves, "Peace, peace, when there is no peace," and it is a kindness to undeceive them. There are also some who forget that the laws of the spiritual world are no less inflexible and inviolable than those of the physical world; that conduct is everything; and that the faith which saves, and which, working by love, makes conduct, is something much deeper and more substantial than the muttering of an unfelt creed, or than the melancholy presumption that to think ourselves saved is by itself a passport into the everlasting habitations.

Jeremiah vi. 14.

There is the judgment and the confidence and the secret.

I. The Judgment. Holy Scripture, while expressing figuratively the Divine mind in the judgment and purpose, and even the surroundings of it, that we may be helped to comprehend all that is meant to be comprehended, also enunciates beneath figure and symbol some distinct and elementary principles of unspeakable value which lie at the root of it.

First. Who are the judged? This question is not so gratuitous as might be supposed. There are those who, just out of a sense of the completeness of the Divine mercy, and of the inviolableness of the Divine covenant, and of the perfectness of the Divine salvation, hold, and strongly hold, that the saved or the righteous—in other words, the Church—will not be judged at all, but will simply be spectators and assessors of the judgment on others. To put it in a different way, where Christ says so emphatically, " He that heareth my word and believeth on Him that sent me, hath everlasting life, and shall not come into condemnation, but is passed from death unto life," by " condemnation " He simply meant "judgment"; *John v. 24.*

something quite different from condemnation, though of course it may end in it. This, it may be shewed, is only in harmony with what St. Paul tells us in the summing up of his argument on justification: "There is now, therefore, no condemnation to them which are in Christ Jesus, who walk not after the flesh, but after the Spirit." This view, however, must be considered in the light of other and fuller scriptures; also in relation to the revelation of the glory of God and the moral necessities of man. St. Paul tells us distinctly in the beginning of the same epistle that in the day "when God shall judge the secrets of men," He will render to "them who, by patient continuance in well-doing, seek for glory and honour and immortality, eternal life"; and again, very clearly, that "we must *all* appear [or be manifested] before the judgment-seat of Christ, that every one may receive the things done in his body according to that he hath done, whether it be good or bad." St. John, at the close of the Apocalypse, tells us of his awful vision: "I saw the dead, small and great, stand before God; and the books were opened, and another book was opened, which is the book of life, and the dead

Romans viii. 1.

Romans ii. 16.

Romans ii. 7.

2 Cor. v. 10.

Rev. xx. 12, 15.

were judged out of those things which were written in the books, according to their works, and whosoever was not written in the book of life was cast into the lake of fire."

In the passage before us the one point is that they are to be in judgment, and yet not to be in terror at it. But if they were to escape judgment altogether, what could be the need of assuring them of the confidence that will then possess them, but which in such a case they would not be in a condition to require? Besides, it is not the usual way of inspired teachers to console us against an ordeal that never can be ours. We shall all be judged—nay, we must all be judged. We shall all be judged, that God may be glorified in those who have believed on Him, as well as glorified on those who have consciously and persistently rejected Him. This will be for the final vindication of the eternal righteousness. We must all be judged, for how in the moral constitution of things can it be otherwise?

Our personal lives as shaping and completing our moral character will then be manifested in a suitable body that shall be prepared for us, and the manifestation will be at once the verdict and the sentence. "The righteous shall shine forth as the sun in the kingdom of their Father." The unprofitable servant shall be cast "into outer darkness:" there shall be weeping and gnashing of teeth. The justice of this is as apparent as are the wisdom and inevitableness of the mode in which it will operate. The great white throne, on which the Judge will be seated, will, it may reverently be gathered from the words of the Old Testament prophet, be of living fire, which will penetrate and illuminate, and purify and consume. To some a baptism of the Holy Ghost and of fire, to others an instrument of self-revelation and despair, it will be the symbol and the vehicle of infinite holiness and truth to the great concourse of all the children of Adam. St. John only here, and alone of the inspired writers (except St. Peter), refers to that day as the day of judgment. Elsewhere it is called "that day," "the last day,' "a day," "a great and terrible day." Let us confess that the mind reels and staggers under any attempt to construct, even imagine, the methods or features of this stupendous assize which our Lord and His apostles have so

Matt. xiii. 93.

Matt. xxv. 30.

Daniel vii. 9.

2 Peter ii. 9.

impressively and solemnly and emphatically and distinctly announced to us as the final winding up and ending of the history of our race on the earth. It is enough to know that we may regard it as more absolutely certain than that the sun will rise to-morrow; that it has been delayed in mercy, that for a while mercy may rejoice against judgment; but that the hour will come when the true mercy will be to pronounce judgment and to dismiss the judged to their supreme reward. It will all be supernatural, for the present laws of time and space and motion and vision, the only laws we know of by experience, will have been superseded by new conditions, of which we know nothing except that they will be ordained of God. It fills the spirit with awe, and, but for the blood which cleanseth from all sin, might paralyse even the believer with terror. The great criminals of the world and the great saints, writers who have polluted generations after them, and writers who have inspired them with lofty and generous ideals, preachers who have turned many to righteousness, and tyrants who have filled hell with their victims, will meet their Judge and know their doom, and the

<small>Rev. xvi. 5.</small> secret utterance of all will be, "Thou art righteous, O Lord, because Thou hast judged thus."

But the apostle tells of the *confidence*: a word which not unfrequently occurs elsewhere in the New Testament, and has for its first meaning freedom of speech. St. John, of course, is here referring to the believer in Christ. The expression suggests the idea that the apostle is recalling the figure in the parable of the final judgment of the heathen world, to which he must once have listened, and which he was not likely ever to forget, in which the Lord, the Righteous Judge, condescends to hold converse with those whom He has to welcome or to banish, and promises to those who shall be found in Him living partakers of His eternal life, that boldness or freedom of speech which at once assures acceptance and utters praise. It could have hardly even occurred to the apostle, with this assurance of their joy, that they could for one moment desire to be kept outside of it. Terror will be impossible. Not a ripple of alarm will ruffle the perfect tranquillity of those who see in that supreme moment Him on Whom they have believed. They will instantly and joyfully recognise in Him the Saviour on Whom, it may be, long ago they cast the burden of their sins, and He cast it behind His back; the Master Whose voice gave them their orders, Whose wisdom directed their footsteps, Whose presence cheered their loneliness, and Whose mercy crowned their labours; the Spouse to Whom they had betrothed themselves in the ineffable blessedness of a mystical but actual life; the Friend to Whom they could take every secret, confide every trouble, whisper every trial, trust in every temptation—whose love, little as they knew of it, rejoiced over them and put them to shame because they had not learnt it more. To be afraid of Him, to be ashamed of Him, to hide themselves from Him, to distrust Him in that wonderful moment for which the Church has been waiting and the Holy Spirit moving, and the Eternal Father counselling, and each individual believer in his best and purest moments, secretly, almost impatiently longing with a desire not to be put into words, should not only be felt unworthy and pusillanimous, derogatory to the faithfulness of God, wounding and dishonouring to the cross and victory of Christ, but it is just impossible for any one who has really found Christ and lived in the light of His love.

This will be made even plainer from the explanation St. John gives of his amazing paradox, "Because as He is, so are we in this world." The literal meaning of this must be, "Because as He (Christ) is eternally, and now in His character as it is known to us, are we even now in this world, out of which indeed He has passed, but in which we still live and serve." It is clear, of course, that the secret of this confidence may have two explanations, each of which is perfectly consistent with the other, each of which represents the one side or half of a most essential whole. One of these explanations may not inexactly be described as what St. Paul might have given—the objective side of the truth. The other is what I think St. John intended, which is the subjective side. Who, for instance, would care or even dare to deny that the true and immovable and evangelical ground of the sinner's peace is his spiritual union with Christ, that union which the Sacraments at once represent, and, when duly received, convey, of which faith takes

Text.

living and joyful, and tenacious hold, which means in the eyes of God a personal and moral identity with Christ—" Who is made unto us wisdom and righteousness and sanctification and redemption ; " on Whom we have cast our sins, and Who has given us in exchange His own perfect righteousness ; in Whom even now, by virtue of our personal and spiritual union with Him, we "stand perfect and complete in all the will of God"? It is, in fact, the substance of St. Paul's own aspiration about himself: " And be found in Him, not having mine own righteousness, which is of the law, but that which is through the faith of Christ, the righteousness which is of God by faith; that I may know Him and the power of His resurrection." It is also the precise doctrine which he laid down in his Epistle to the Romans : " Being justified by faith, let us have peace with God through our Lord Jesus Christ." This is the faith of the Gospel and perhaps the central truth of it; and this freedom with which Christ makes us free we must never let go for an hour. But the context makes it clear that this was not the truth the apostle of love had in his mind when he penned these wonderful words. He was

1 Cor. i. 30.

Col. iv. 12.

Phil. iii. 9.

Rom. v. 1.

thinking of Christ's character, not of His satisfaction; and of the one quality which at once comprehends, illuminates, and beatifies it—Love. All through the chapter he has been expounding and impressing love. In the verse immediately before the text, he had written, "We have known and believed the love that God hath to [in] us; God is love, and he that dwelleth in love dwelleth in God, and God in him." Then the thought expands, and moves into a higher region and more distant future. Love, he seems to say, and then even judgment itself shall have no terror for you. Perfect love casts out fear. He that feareth is not made perfect in love. But in that day you will be made perfect in love. For even now love is your nature, your effort, your desire; and as your Head is in the perfect love of heaven, so are you now, by His grace and benediction, like Him even on earth. In the day of judgment no earthly ties will distract you, no human activities dissipate you, no idolatries divide your affections, no roots of sin paralyse your will. The character of your Lord shall then finally and supremely be your character. Faith, which has hitherto worked by love, and manifested its trueness therein, shall be rewarded by it. "We love Him because He first loved us," shall be the new song of the redeemed. *1 John iv. 19.*

There is another reason yet (have I not kept the best for the last?) for the victory of love in that tremendous day. Let me give it in the apostle's own words: "Beloved, now are we the sons of God, and it doth not yet appear what we shall be, but we know that when He shall appear we shall be like Him, for we shall see Him as He is." *1 John iii. 2.* This idea was familiar to St. Paul, and in his Second Epistle to the Corinthians he presses the wonderful truth that even now the contemplation of Christ shall produce resemblance to Him, though we behold that glory as in a glass darkly, with the imperfections and interruptions incidental to our life here. But in the great and awful day when the sign of the Son of Man appears in heaven, and He comes with clouds to judgment, there will be no veil between His unclouded brightness and the glorified spirits of His elect. The vision of the Judge will mean the transfiguration of His people: to see Him face to face in His eternal and yet redeeming glory will be to love as He loves, and to welcome as He welcomes. We cannot, indeed, presume to anticipate the bliss of that moment, but if perfect love is to cast out fear, the sense of past sin and unworthiness shall be swallowed up for ever in the heavenly city whose walls are salvation and its gates praise. Now our humble petition too often has to be, "Create in me a clean heart, O God, and renew a right spirit within me." Then what a burst of song will break forth from the millions and millions of the redeemed in the House of their Father: "Unto Him which loved and washed us from our sins in His own blood, and hath made us kings and priests unto God and the Father, be glory and dominion both now and for ever. Amen."

Ps. vi. 10.

Rev. i. 5, 6.

St. John in the preceding chapter (iii. 3), speaks of "this hope in [on] Him"; and St. Paul has the same thought when, in almost the last letter he wrote, he describes the attitude of the Church as "looking for that blessed hope and the glorious appearing of the great God and our Saviour Jesus Christ"; and once more he writes to one of the churches in Asia: "which is Christ in you, the hope of glory." This hope must be cherished and fed if it is to

Titus ii. 13.

Col. i. 27.

be to us all that it is meant to be, in helping us to rightly anticipate that day of judgment before it comes, tranquilly to meet it when it does come. Is there any conceivable way more natural or more helpful than that of entertaining Him in our hearts, of being ready and even eager, in the moments when He comes to visit us, to hold living fellowship with Him, to unburden our cares to Him in the effort of a true devotion, sometimes to sit and think of Him (which is the heart's secret worship) as the end and promise, and reward and consummation of all? Occasionally Christians complain that they seldom see His face or enjoy His presence. The question occurs, Whose fault is that? There is a passage in the Canticles that carries a deserved rebuke to some who should be in a greater haste to condemn themselves than to complain of their Lord. "I sleep, but my heart waketh. It is the voice of my beloved that knocketh, saying, 'Open to me, my sister, my love, my undefiled! I have put off my coat; how shall I put it on? I have washed my feet; how shall I defile them? I opened to my beloved, but my beloved had withdrawn himself, and was gone.' *Canticles v. 2-6.*

I sought him, but I could not find him; I called him, but he gave me no answer."

There are also those to whom the thought of meeting their Lord has neither rapture nor consolation in it; not that they are impenitent or insincere, but that they are content to remain on a low level of spiritual vitality. The life within them stagnates rather than grows; they will be saved, but there cannot be for them an abundant entrance into the everlasting kingdom. When Christ promised to those who loved Him and kept His word, *John xiv. 23.* "My Father will love him, and we will come unto him and make our abode with him," by the coming He meant something that was to be recognised and felt; by the abiding, the ineffable fruition of a Divine fellowship. Sometimes it seems to one that the greatest peril and disgrace of real Christians is laziness. It is laziness that makes short prayers, a neglected Bible, works that are dead, love that is tepid, interrupted fellowship, and growth stunted, from lack of living water at the roots. The question of questions is, Now, Lord, what is my hope? Surely my hope is even in Thee? The reply of replies must be: "When wilt thou come unto me? I will walk in my house with a perfect heart." *Ps. ci. 2.*

What we most wish for is a test of our real character that cannot be explained away. To how many of us is the coming of Christ our secret hope and stay?

St. John, however, is very careful not to suffer us to imagine that this hope is a mere barren sentiment, without motive, or effort, or result. What is to come out of it if it is the right sort of hope, and not merely a selfish desire to be rid of the troubles of life, is a continuous struggle after the image of His holiness. "Every man that hath this hope in [on] Him purifieth himself even as He is pure." *1 John iii. 3.*
Here is at once the measure of our struggle and the instrument of it. Christ's perfection is to be our model; self-purification—what is elsewhere described as "working out our own salvation"—is to be the continuous and unwearied way to it. Among the evil dispositions from which we are to purify ourselves are, surely, first and foremost, those that wound, and chill, and vitiate love? Every root of bitterness; every habit of unkind, or uncharitable, or sarcastic speech; haste to think, and even

more to pronounce, evil; all proneness to place or leave a stumbling-block in our brother's way, are absolutely fatal to the cherishing of this hope, which means the being admitted into the Father's house, where all the children of one blessed family love and are loved, without soil or taint, or reserve or grudging; where He Who is love will give to His children fully to partake of His own nature; where selfishness will have ceased to be possible; and where to walk in love, as Christ has loved us, will be at once the rule and freedom of our lives.

Not that this love means a feeble complacency with evil, or a condoning of what we know to be wrong for peace sake, or silence when we ought to rebuke sin, or indifference when it is our duty to prevent it. Christ is always our example, and sometimes even He reproved those whom He loved best at the moment when they thought to be serving Him. God Who is Love is also a consuming fire, and the love which has nothing of burning in it is not the love of God.

Once more, there is the Vision of Love. "We shall see Him as He is," says St. John.

In the Revelation we have an account of what the apostle had then seen; but it is all type and figure, so that it does not help us much to know what we shall see when the "King in His beauty" is before our eyes. But the emblem of fire, with which His eyes will gaze and His feet move and His face beam on us, indicates the penetrating, irresistible, consuming holiness which He will come at once to demand and represent and bestow.

He will be different to every one in that great concourse, for the faculty of sight will infinitely vary, and every soul as it gazes on Him will have its own conception and amazement, its own untold gladness or its own self-reproaching anguish. His love—and He will be the very embodiment and ideal of love to those who have received and desired and imitated it—will be a revelation of wonderful and delightful beauty; to those who have disbelieved or despised or rejected it, it will bring at once a vindication of the righteousness which simply pronounces on them their self-chosen banishment and a discovery of their tremendous loss of a treasure so priceless and so dear. To see Christ and know Him for our own Kinsman, and plead Him for our salvation, and to welcome Him as our Master, and to crown Him as our Lord, with hearts that can perfectly love and wills that can instantly obey, and minds that can grasp Him, and consciences that can taste the full healing of His precious blood, will indeed be the beginning of a new creation, when the wonder-ful words are quite fulfilled : "Old things are passed away behold all things are become new." To those who find out what they have lost, and remember that they have lost it, not through ignorance, but through unbelief, the sense of their loss and their sin will surely be woe enough without our adding in imagination other sorrow to it! One glimpse of His beauty to help them to understand what it is that they have rejected; and then, with the last recollection of Him as one in whose face was the look of an infinite pity but an inflexible justice, to go away into the darkness to see His face no more. Can there be any sorrow to compare with that?

2 Cor. v. 17.

IN THE LIFE TO COME

" When round his head the aureole glows
And he is clothed in white,
I'll take his hand, and go with him
To the deep wells of light,
As unto a stream we will step down,
And bathe there in God's sight."

D. G. ROSSETTI.

IX

IN THE LIFE TO COME

"*The bride, the Lamb's wife.*"—REVELATION xxi. 9.

WE are on our way home; and every hour brings us nearer to it. Its light will be the vision of God, and its reward His image; its gladness His love, its society His saints. If we really believe this, and with any intenseness care for it, it is simply impossible that we should not sometimes muse on the nature of its blessedness, and conjecture as to the conditions of its life. "If the future be not a hope, it will be a fear." There need be no presumptuous curiosity in desiring to understand what Holy Scripture, mystically, no doubt, yet actually, has told us of it. The book which, more than any other, lets us into its secrets, is the only book to which the special promise is given, *Canon Ainger.*

<small>Rev. i. 3.</small> "Blessed is he that readeth, and they that hear the words of this prophecy." It is not an arrogant pulling away at the thick curtain, which is meant to shut out from us the invisible world, that inspires us to look not only at the things which are seen, but at those which are not seen; to seek them, and not to despise them; to come apart from the tumult and distraction of the world, in dutiful and yet <small>Text.</small> eager obedience to the angel's invitation, "Come hither, I will show thee the bride, the Lamb's wife." But to see the bride is to behold her <small>Sermons, p. 365.</small> Lord. Nevertheless, as Dr. Ker has finely cautioned us, let us recognise our limitations, and accept them. Then we shall be protected at once from disappointment and a vain speculativeness, akin to disrespect. St. John himself, who had seen and learned more of the world to come than any of the sons of men, gives us them, in what are perhaps his final <small>1 John iii. 2.</small> words, "It doth not yet appear"—or it hath not yet been manifested—"what we shall be."

On these points, for instance, our ignorance is at once complete and insuperable. Where what we call heaven as a locality will be found to be we know not; and no telescope that was ever invented, or ever will be, can find that out. Whether or no some distant orb, far away in the galaxy of worlds, will be our future place of habitation, or, as some would be glad to know, this present earth of ours, purged as with fire from all stains of sin and cruelty and pain, is to be made a new heavens and a new earth, in which the elect of God shall share His bliss and righteousness, eye hath not seen nor ear heard. We do not know, and it does not matter. Nor again has it been made clear to us, except in the most general language, what will be the spiritual body which we shall put on at the resurrection, in its shape, its laws, its organs. It may be that the body, which our Lord assumed during the forty days between His resurrection and ascension, is to be the pattern and type of ours. In that body, as we read, He appeared and disappeared, as it pleased Him; He ate and drank; He inspired an awe and sense of majesty such as before His death His apostles never seem to have felt about Him; in His ascension into heaven He transcended at His will the usual laws of our material being. They knew Him again, when He wished to be known again, and He was a stranger when He wished to be a stranger. Whether this was His normal condition, or only a transitional one to meet their needs and condescend to their infirmities, the Gospels do not explain.

In that home which we think we desire, and to which we are journeying, what we call the conditions of time and space will surely have ceased to be. Time is an accident of our planetary condition. The glorified bodies, with which the resurrection will endow us, will probably have new forces for movement and duty and sustentation such as we cannot imagine now. Once more, in that great multitude of every kindred and nation and people and tongue, if they are to sing together the new song, and to mingle in the saintly and joyous fellowship of those who have washed their robes and made them white in the blood of the Lamb, they must have one speech and one language in which to praise God and edify one another. But on this, too, there is silence. It may well be that there will be other ways than that of speech for communicating thoughts and enjoying intercourse; but if speech is to continue, and it seems incredible that it should not, a

IN THE LIFE TO COME

new language will be needed, and will doubtless be given by Him whose promise is declared, "Behold I make all things new." *Rev. xxi. 5.*

Of one thing, however, with all these uncertainties, which are comparatively of little consequence, we may be perfectly certain, and this is of unspeakable consequence. Christ's love will contrive, and ordain, and provide, and console for all whom He shall finally have rescued from the storms of this troublesome world into the home and fruition of God. "The Lamb which is in the midst of the throne *Rev. vii. 17.* shall feed (shepherd) them; and shall lead them unto fountains of living waters; and God shall wipe away all tears from their eyes."

First, let us consider some of the reasons which go to explain the causes of the special manifestation of Christ's love to His people, when they are safely at home with Him in glory, then proceed to show what this love will imply and bestow for those who receive it; and finally, with all reverence and humility, inquire in what modes and by what instrumentalities the manifestation of that love is likely to be made. Reverence touched with devoutness, and stirred by a noble hope, shall pilot us on our voyage, as we move into the solemn twilight, with its far horizon tipped with gold. Should the privilege be also claimed as a duty, there is nothing strange in it, if the love of Christ, felt and returned, will be the joy of heaven. To speculate wildly, and then to dogmatise harshly, is an error, almost amounting to a sin. To gaze eagerly, timidly, but earnestly, across the clouded borderland, and with an open Bible and an obedient heart, to try to think out some at least of the things which God hath prepared for them that love Him, is a reasonable, even a beautiful solace for those who sometimes need a sip of heavenly cordial for the tired hours of a waning life; who, on their way to see the King in His beauty, wish to know more exactly what that beauty will be.

The first explanation of Christ's tender love to His Church in her glorified and sinless condition may be thought to be that there will be nothing on her part to chill His affection, or to move His regret, or to disappoint His hopes, as now too often is the case, when the taint of sin defiles even the saintliest nature, and when the cares and possessions of earth make even the believer's love wax cold. The poet's sentence will then have become impossible: "The best in me that sees the worst in me, and groans over it." The Church will then be worthy of His love, through the worthiness He has Himself given to her; He will have presented her to Himself "a glorious Church, not having spot or wrinkle or any such thing," but "holy and without blemish." But His love will mean His joy. "As a bridegroom rejoiceth over the bride, so shall thy God rejoice over thee." *Dante.*

Isaiah lxii 5.

Another consideration, in connection with the one just named, though not quite identical with it, is that, in the ransomed and glorified Church, the Saviour will recognise the spoils of His conflict, and welcome the result of His incarnation, and behold the triumph of His cross. The saints were given to Him by His Father before the worlds were made. They have been often tempted, corrupted, erring, disobedient. But He has Himself washed them from their sins in His own blood; He has made them more than conquerors through faith and grace. He has kept them in the world, and brought them out of it; and they will then be in a sense what they have never been before, His for ever. They are at last at home in their Father's house, and no man shall pluck them out of the Father's hand. Our human nature, without its frailty and sinfulness, is Christ's, and it is human to love with a very special love those for whom we have done, and sacrificed, and suffered much, if in the end all is not in vain, and our heart's desire is accomplished. Each one of His elect will be made to feel His love as if he were the only one loved. Each with his past history, his wonderful deliverances, his merciful chastenings, and his last struggle, will be safe and sinless at home.

Another consideration may stir the expression of Christ's love to us, though the ground of it is due to His grace and help alone. His own parables justify the application of a law which lies deep at the root of human conduct. When the King, in the judgment of the heathen world, welcomes as beloved of the Father into everlasting life those who unknowingly have ministered to Himself in ministering to their brethren; when the master of a household, travelling into a far country, gives his servants whom he is about to leave talents to trade with

according to their several ability, and on his
return praises and rewards those who have
been faithful to their trust, whether great or
small; when the great apostle of faith, who
counted himself less than the least of the
apostles, could at the end of his career look
forward confidently to the crown of righteousness which the Lord, the righteous Judge,
would give him—for had he not fought a good
fight, and finished his course, and kept the
faith—is there anything presumptuous or un-
reasonable in the expectation that, when our
Master and Lord permits us to see what we
have done for Him and by Him during our life
on earth, obscurely or visibly, by cups of cold
water, or the agonies of an awful martyrdom,
by kindness to the poor, or patience with
children, or dutifulness to the old, or ministra-
tions to the sick—sometimes, it may be, by
turning many to righteousness, always by the
irresistible power of a meek goodness—will
not our Lord love us for this, as we love each
other for it; and will not He tell us so, and
tell others so, in ways and language of His
own; and will not the sight of what He has
enabled us to do, when we stand before Him,

with the spiritual children which He Himself has given us, stir Him, with the very hands nailed for our redemption to the cross, to crown us with the crown we have earned, to solace us with the love that we desire? "The righteous Judge"—what a sentence that is! Polycarp and Blondina, Brainerd and Martyn, with the great multitude that no man can number, will one day know, and we shall know it too, all that His gratitude means.

<small>2 Tim. iv. 8.</small>

One other reason let me give; perhaps it is the best of all. It is plain from our Lord's parting discourse in the upper chamber how He himself longed with an infinite desire to have His disciples with Him in His glory. From the nature of things it is evident how much more the Church will be to Him than ever He will be to the Church, just because His love is infinite, being the love of God, and hers, though ever growing through all the ages, is finite, for it is the love of a creature. "I go to prepare a place for you. If I go and prepare a place for you, I will come again and receive you unto myself, that where I am ye may be also." "Father, I will that they also whom Thou hast given me be with me where I am,

<small>John xiv. 2. 3.</small>

<small>John xvii. 24.</small>

that they may behold my glory which Thou hast given me, for Thou lovedst me before the foundation of the world." It is a wonderful truth, that should indeed thaw and quicken us, and put us to shame, but there is no contradicting it, that Christ will always love us far, far more than we shall ever love Him. Heaven will be more heavenly to Him, the Incarnate Saviour, when His Church is there to behold and share His glory. Heaven can be heaven only to those to whom Christ's love is precious now.

> "*Ce n'est pas dans le ciel qu'on trouve Dieu. c'est en Dieu qu'on trouve le ciel.*" — *Godet.*

But what is it that His love will then bestow on us, and in which the final manifestation of it will be made perfect?

First, there will be provision, ample, regular, and complete. Nor is this a superfluous consideration, for we shall be creatures still, everlastingly creatures, drawing every breath from His sustaining and directing will; in Him then, as now, living, and moving, and having our being. This thought is perhaps sufficiently contained in the promise to those who had come out of the great tribulation, but of course applicable to all. "The Lamb which is in the midst of the throne shall feed them"—(here "feed," in the original, gives the idea of shepherding)—"and shall lead them to fountains of living waters." Another figure, which conveys this truth in another way, is at the close of the Apocalypse, where "he showed me a pure river of water of life, clear as crystal, proceeding out of the throne of God and of the Lamb. In the midst of the street of it, and on either side of the river, there was the tree of life, which bare twelve manner of fruits, and yielded her fruits every month, and the leaves of the tree were for the healing of the nations." Whether the physical life of the glorified body will need refreshment and invigoration by food, it is impossible to say, though that it will be incapable of eating and drinking is hardly to be gathered, in case there is any analogy between our glorified body and the Lord's. For we read of Him, that as a visible token of His risen life, "To us who did eat and drink with them after He rose from the dead." Twice also before His death He glanced at the life to come for His disciples, in words which do not

Rev. xxii. 1, 2.

Acts x. 41.

make it extravagant to conjecture, that in this respect there may be some resemblance between the earthly and the glorified organism. St. Luke records how, just before His Passion, He announced to His disciples, "I appoint unto you a kingdom, as my Father hath appointed unto me, that ye may eat and drink at my table in my kingdom and sit on thrones judging the twelve tribes of Israel." St. Matthew also records: "I will not drink henceforth of this fruit of the vine, until that day when I drink it new with you in my Father's kingdom." *Luke xxii. 29, 30.* *Matt. xxvi. 29.*

All this, however, is among the things unrevealed, and which do not particularly concern us now. We are, at any rate, certain that in the sense of need that will aggravate with care, or fatigue with toil, or mortify with want, or corrode with sickness, "they shall hunger no more, neither thirst any more." There, as much as now, the promise will hold good: "My God shall supply all your need according to His riches in glory by Christ Jesus." But about other things we are perfectly assured that the Good Shepherd will provide for the flock, which He has gone abroad *Phil. iv. 19.*

on the wild and desolate mountains to snatch from the ravening wolf, and to bring back for ever unto the still waters and green pastures of the heavenly fold. They are these three—grace, truth, and safety. In the heavenly country we shall still be temples of the Holy Ghost; still be blessed, and healed, and edified, and consoled by Him. But there and then there will be no obstruction on our part to the full inflowing of His light, and love, and power into every nerve and fibre of our spiritual being. No longer will it be possible for us to quench or to grieve Him, or to sin against His love. There as here, there will be among the redeemed infinite varieties of capacity for receiving His grace; and it is probable that all through the ages to come this capacity will be indefinitely increased. But the Lord will lead us to the fountains of waters, and, thirsting blessedly, we shall be abundantly satisfied with the river of His pleasures.

This constant replenishing of our spiritual powers must surely mean for us a continual growth in the perception and fruition of the Divine life. From grace to grace, and from strength to strength, the love of our Incarnate Lord will conduct us, and thus our joy, because our holiness, will grow. Truth, also, He will provide for us; and what a vista of noble delight this thought opens up to the soul! The Word of God is Himself the Truth. Here there are, even to the keenest-witted and most studious, and most intellectual of the race, breaks, interruptions, scanty opportunities; inevitable and mortifying limitations both for the acquisition and the imparting of knowledge, of whatever kind it may be. When one student dies, a discovery it may be on the point of being made, and that would have illuminated and blessed the entire human race, is lost; and centuries may pass before the extinguished torch is lit again. Whether the knowledge be of God Himself as revealed in His holy Word, or of His marvellous and manifold works as exhibited in nature, or of His government of the world as portrayed in history, or of the powers and characteristics of His greatest handiwork—man; how little does any of us know now, how imperfectly at the best do we know it! As life goes on we shed and drop much of our accumulated treasure;

at the end the wise man's cynicism too often justifies itself in our own experience. Not only is "much study" felt to be "a weariness of the flesh," but have we been studying, as we ought, the things best worth knowing?

Ecc. xii. 12.

One of our beautiful and edifying employments in the life to come will surely be the acquisition of knowledge, of all knowledge that can dignify, and interest, and sanctify the glorified soul. There will be no mental indolence, no sour jealousy, no grudging of merit, no puny contempt of any sort of truth. There will be time enough, and strength enough, and opportunity enough, and capacity enough. While then, as now, each mind will differ from every other in taste, and aim, and capacity, no one will be destitute of a thirst for knowledge, no one content without the glory of acquiring it. Those of course will make the best start who, while on earth, have disciplined and cultivated their minds as a talent for God, and in the motive for His glory. But our Lord will go before us, and make for us a way into the higher regions of truth and goodness, and we shall feel that He exhibits His love to us in so doing. He Who was the patient, deep, too often misunderstood and provoked Teacher here on earth, Who now and then could not help saying, in the moment of a wounded surprise, "Why do ye not understand my speech?" will *John viii. 43.* have docile pupils, and eager hearers, then.

One other thing His love will be careful to include in this provision for His people. He will protect them, and they shall lie down safely from the fear of evil. Death and hell will be cast into the lake of fire. Into that city "there *Rev. xxi. 27.* shall in no wise enter anything that defileth, neither worketh abomination, or maketh a lie," "and there shall be no more curse." This is a *Rev. xxii. 3.* thought of unspeakable repose, not only for ourselves but for those whom we love, if possible, better than ourselves; and it is a joy that must kindle in the heart of the Lord Jesus. For ourselves, we remember "let him *1 Cor. x. 12.* that thinketh he standeth take heed lest he fall." The depths of Satan, the deceitfulness of sin, the original inherited flaw in our own nature, the presence of evil in the ways and children of this world are ever with us, and compel us constantly to be on our guard. But for others, too, we sometimes have to watch and fear, often with a sense of wretched helplessness;

and our chief comfort is, that they are dearer to the Lord than to us; that He must be more bent on saving them than we can be; and that our poignant, sometimes our intolerable anxiety, He shares with us, and looks down on our affliction with a holy sympathy. For the soul we would protect and guard may have passed out of childhood, may have made its own friendships and chosen its own path. The child can be protected in one way; one not a child needs another way, not always easy to discover or enforce. If the soul that we would fain save has a certain attraction to and even desire for the evil from which we would guard it, we seem to see it wandering over a glacier, with an awful crevasse opening at its feet. We can do nothing but shut our eyes, and wait, and hope, and pray, remembering that our child is also a child of God and a sheep which Christ has bought with His blood. But the suspense and consciousness of the crisis sometimes amount to an agony. That sort of agony will be for ever over within the gates and walls of Emmanuel's land.

His love will find us service, and just the service for which our lives here will have most suitably framed us, and which our several gifts, and capacity, and experience will best enable us to do. "His servants shall serve Him." There is no detail here, but the fact is sufficient. It is not explained what that service will be, but the principle that the life to come will mean continuous and edifying activity, should inspire us now with a fresh motive for the exact and conscientious fulfilment of our earthly obligations. "The child is father of the man." The labourer on earth will one day be the saint in glory. We know not if with new organs of motion we shall wing our flight to other worlds as heralds of the one everlasting gospel. The book which tells so much of the character which qualifies for heaven, and of the love which constitutes it, is silent, deliberately silent, as to the occupations and ministries, and economy of the heavenly life. This is certain, that in that sentence of the prophet, "Thou shalt call Thy walls Salvation and Thy gates Praise," we are to see that all the activities of the heavenly life, whatever they may be found to be, will be one long service of thanksgiving for the salvation which has been bestowed on us by

Rev. xxiii. 3.

Wordsworth.

Isaiah lx. 18.

the redeeming love of the Lamb that was slain.

Among the rewards named by Christ in His parables for faithful service here, is honourable service in the world to come. The apostles were to judge the twelve tribes of Israel; the faithful stewards of the talents and pounds were to have the function of government and power.

Few motives should be more animating, and few hopes more exhilarating, than the motive of doing our best with our earthly tasks now, that we may be counted worthy of place and duty in the world to come. When we understand that cheerfulness and diligence, and exactness and perseverance, and intelligence and single-mindedness, with even the humblest duties now, may be laying up treasure for us in the life to come, it gives a new dignity to labour and a fresh honourableness to life.

Once more, Christ's love will mean comfort, and a comfort it is not possible for us to receive now. "Are the consolations of God small with thee?" is indeed a question always worth asking, and to honest souls which know something of their inner history, it seldom comes

Job xv. 11.

without a subtle reproach. But there are
consolations on earth suitable for the sorrows
of earth, and there will be consolations in glory
commensurate with the joy of it. "As one *Isaiah lxvi. 13.*
whom his mother comforteth, so will I comfort
you, and ye shall be comforted in Jerusalem;"
this is the prophet's message. "And God shall *Rev. vii. 17.*
wipe away all tears from their eyes," is the
climax of the consolation of St. John. Indeed,
there will be much to comfort us about in that
supreme hour. For memory will be awfully
quick and tenacious, and the heart will tremble
with sensitive love, and conscience will be
right in front of the Incarnate Holiness; and
the tears, all the tears, from off all faces, will
the pierced hand of the crucified, glorified Lord
gently, tenderly, completely wipe away.

Think of the disappointments that will there
meet us, and, but for Christ's love, lacerate us;
and from which no harpings of a myriad harps,
no melody from a million voices could heal
or deliver us, save the face and the voice of
our revealed King. The cruellest of all disappointments is that of parents with children;
when the solace they had looked for is denied,
the confidence they had coveted is given to a

stranger; when the parents' God is not their God, when the deepest, saddest loneliness that the human heart can know is found to be that of going down to the grave, with a heart in pain, though it refuses to speak of its sorrow, a hope extinguished like a torch plunged into water, but not so that any one else could discover its bitterness or assuage its grief. To miss our children's love and duty on earth is bad enough, especially at the moment when we had so often looked for it; but what will it be if, when we look on the bright throng all around us and seek eagerly for them, it be discovered they are not there! Is there any sorrow like unto that sorrow? It ought to be a sorrow, and it will be. But that sorrow, that disappointment is the Saviour's as well, and for more than we mourn for. The tears He wept over a Jerusalem that He could die for but might not save, are tears typical of the travail of His redeeming heart over a great multitude of single obdurate souls, all down the river of time.

From these tears, so beautiful, reasonable, necessary, He will certainly deliver us; how, we cannot say. There will be the tears that will come from the thoughts of our sins, which, when we first see the Saviour, will doubtless seem more sinful, more cruel, more unpardonable than ever. The body of sin will have been dropped in the grave; but assuredly there will be a moral continuity in the invisible history of the human spirit. Though the wounds that sin made will be healed, the marks of the scars may remain, in a sense, for ever.

It will be the sight of the Lamb as it had been slain that will then prove our instant, our wonderful, our entire consolation. To doubt the sufficiency of His blood would be to do grave dishonour to His Incarnate Person and atoning sacrifice. If He forgives us, if He has washed us from our sins, and made us kings and priests to God, we may forgive ourselves, and be clothed in the garments washed in blood, and begin the new song, which all eternity we shall never weary of singing, "Worthy is the Lamb that was slain." *Rev. v. 12.*

Once more, He will comfort us about our mistakes; and there are few things in which thoughtful and generous souls are more reluctant to forgive or comfort themselves. There are all sorts of mistakes in the world; and some which have been hastily and eagerly censured as mistakes, afterwards turn out not to have been mistakes at all, but even splendid successes. There are generous mistakes and there are base mistakes, mistakes about which it is enough to affirm that we are only human; mistakes which, whenever we think of them, sting us with a shame that burns. The worst, the most corroding mistakes, are those that parents make about their children, when they are using opportunities and inviting influences, and offering companionship, for a period short, plastic, awfully appreciative of good or evil, never to be got back when once gone. A mistake that sends a child to a bad school, or places him under the custody of an evil influence, or contrives companionship for worldly interests, or connives at indulgences, or relaxations, imprudent, though not noxious, for good nature or peace sake, may one day prove to have been a mistake so serious, so far-reaching, so deplorable, that conscience calls it a sin; and over regrets and efforts and prudence that have become useless, and a firmness that irritates instead of impressing the will, are written those tremendous words which sound the knell to so many human hearts—Too late. To be comforted about these mistakes, and to see, for the first time, how the kindness and wisdom of God have anticipated and mitigated the consequences of our folly, and have even made them work together for good, will surely be almost the highest bliss the human soul can taste. We all err, and we all need indulgence in turn both from God and each other. But some of us, in the providence of God, have had circumstances made for us in which wisdom is singularly needful, and especially hard. Most men can be wise after the event—supernaturally wise also about their neighbour's business. But the heart that loves will often be sensitive and self-reproaching in proportion to its love. The Lamb that is in the midst of the throne, King as well as Saviour, will know how to deliver us from the remorse of the irrecoverable past.

But by what method will Christ's love arrange and fashion all this for us? "The bride is the Lamb's wife." How will He nourish and cherish the Church which is His own body, as her Spouse, and Head, and Saviour? Some of these methods, it is not irreverent to say, we can guess and anticipate now. Some are among those secret things

Text.

which belong unto the Lord, and which He will reveal in His time.

The first and greatest method of apprehending and receiving His love will be the sudden vision of His revealed glory. "They shall see His face." "We shall see Him as He is." What that face, what the seeing of it will be, no lips of man can tell. But it will be a lifetime lived in a moment; the rising of the sun without clouds on a storm-tossed soul struggling with the darkness; the glance of an ineffable love on souls longing for it, and at last satisfied with it; the contact with a holiness which will make the impenitent dumb, but set the hearts of the righteous on fire. That Presence will ever encompass us. There may be for aught we know occasional and solitary communions with Him. But we can never go where He is not, never feel to have lost Him in those vast and shining spaces irradiated all through with the splendour of His glory. The Lamb in the midst of the throne will be like the sun shining in his might at noonday. He will live in our hearts, and His name will be on our foreheads.

Then there will be the worship of heaven,

Rev. xxii. 4.
1 John iii. 2.

about which it is written: "I saw no temple therein, for the Lord God Almighty and the Lamb are the temple thereof." *Rev. xxi. 22.* That worship, so far as the adoring thankful praise of redeemed souls is to be understood by it, will indeed convey to the hearts of the worshippers, as well as to the throne of Him Whom they worship, the thrill of an infinite love. Nothing deepens, stirs, gladdens, transfigures the soul like passionate, absorbed, adoring worship; unworthy as any worship we offer here is to be described thus. There, however it will bring summer into the soul. It will be so intelligent, so continuous, so full of memories, so wondering at itself, so conscious of salvation, though with no confession in it; so conscious also of dependence, though there will be no sigh about temptation, no bitter cry of a heart in peril of death at the approach of a destroyer. All praise, all worship, all communion—no thought, no taint of self.

Then there will be the fellowship of saints to represent and convey Christ's love to us— nay, to be the mouthpiece and channel of it. What greetings, what welcomes, what tender embraces, what awed and yet blissful introductions there will be of saint to saint, and martyr to martyr, and teacher to teacher, and friend to friend! Speaking in the language of men, this alone will take no little time for us to make the acquaintance and hear the voices and learn the histories of only a few in that countless white-robed throng. There will be no cold reserve, no chilling silence, no checking of eager veneration, no pushing away those who would thankfully sit at the feet of the saints and masters of the past. We shall all have to give and to receive, all to question and answer, all to observe and wonder, all to listen and learn. But every one will, after his own fashion, and according to his past life and conversation, represent and reflect and convey Christ to his brethren. Christ will see Himself in every one, and every one will see Christ in every one else. Each will be beautiful with his own individual and separate beauty; but Christ will be the ornamentation and glory of all.

Oh, what the Christian martyrs of all the successive ages, from Nero's Palatine gardens to Madagascar and Uganda, will have to tell each other; how those who have written for the truth, and those who have given their lives for it; soldiers like Gordon, and bishops like Hannington, shall meet Polycarp and Latimer; to speak of the wondrous tender love that dulled the sharpness of the axe, and made the lion's roar like the music of a child singing; and we shall stand outside on the edge of the crowd, thankful to have our standing place there, just to listen to them. Christ is for all, and the saints are for each other; and what the grace and edification, and delight, and power of that heavenly society will prove, surely we must first be there to discover.

Then, there will be the ministry of angels, to whom we owe so much more now than we are permitted to know, to whom, then, we shall be better able to express our gratitude for what they have been to us, and done for us, in moments of helplessness and uncertainty, and even despair. We are to spend eternity in their company. If they minister to us here, because we are heirs of salvation, shall we not commune with them there, when we are heirs of glory? We are a little lower than them now —perhaps shall always be. But we are sure they love us, and we may be well assured that we shall love them. They, too, though not members of Christ's Incarnate body as we are, ministered to Him in His flesh, minister before Him in His glory. They will surely be also ministers of His love and goodness to us, though in ways that we know not. We must wait to understand.

As to other unrevealed ways in which the love of Christ will communicate itself to us, while we may reverently suppose that in the nature of things there will be such, it is wiser and humbler not to attempt to penetrate into them. God fulfils Himself in many ways; and of all conceivable things none is less conceivable than that a glorified spirit should have occasion to feel disappointment either as to the joy of heaven or the love of Christ.

In conclusion, let us observe how that wonderful sentence: "The Lamb is the light thereof," may be used as a promise that when this life is over, with all its puzzles and disappointments and mistakes, Christ will interpret to each of us the plan and the purpose and the sense and the way of it, and help us understand as we cannot understand here, the love that now underlies and overrules it all. "Thou

Rev. xxi. 23.

Deut. viii. 2, 3.

shalt remember all the way which the Lord thy God led thee these forty years in the wilderness, to humble thee and to prove thee; to know what was in thy heart, whether thou wouldest keep His commandments or no. And He humbled thee and suffered thee to hunger, and fed thee with manna, which thou knowest not, neither did thy fathers know, that He might make thee know that man doth not live by bread alone, but by every word that proceedeth out of His mouth doth man live."

There are many questions we ask ourselves now about things we cannot understand. Affliction is one of them. Some people are always being afflicted, and with afflictions that scorch like fire. There are not a few who whisper to themselves, and not without cause, "I am the man who have seen affliction by the rod of His wrath," though for "wrath" they would substitute "love." Well, occasionally such afflicted souls confess to themselves that they need it all, whether to subdue pride or to overcome the love of the world in their hearts; or (lofty privilege) to be able to comfort others also with the consolation which they themselves have received of God. When we

Lamentations iii. 1.

see Him we shall know all about it, for He will tell us in some way of His own. Till then we will tarry His leisure and wait for His appearing, and expect His·light.

Another thought of unspeakable comfort is the thought of Christ's love in the· life to come in sheltering us from what will be for ever passed, the pavilion of His presence from the "pride of man," and from "the strife of tongues." Those who have any public duty to perform, or have any difficult place to fill, often at the moment when they are doing their duty with most singleness of heart and purity of motive, stir into fury the indignation of those who happen to be affected by it, and have to bear misrepresentation and condemnation, usually from those totally ignorant of the circumstances, which come on us like rough blows on the cheek from a soiled hand—blows that can neither be acknowledged or returned. Manhood bears such things as silently as may be; faith accepts them as a reward for duty, and charity waits for its reprisals in coals of fire. Further, there will be many beautiful reconciliations and handshakings before the throne of God. Milton and Juxon

Psalm xxxi. 20.

will meet; Baxter and Beveridge; Bossuet and Fénelon; Keble and Arnold; all washed in the same blood, radiant in the same righteousness, confessing the same Saviour, singing one song. How glad they will be to meet and understand each other; how sorry they will be, if there can be regret in heaven, that they did not understand each other better on earth!

Oh, that we would try and anticipate this now, while there is time to save the Church from division, and the world from scandal. There is no monopoly of truth or of goodness for any of us. While to our own Master we stand or fall, by love we should serve one another. Again, when we are there we shall, I suppose, be filled with a sense of completeness, and yet of incompleteness. We shall awake after His likeness and be satisfied with it. Yet who will ever feel that he loves Christ as He deserves to be loved, or serves Him as He claims to be served, or knows Him as He desires to be known, or resembles Him as our hope is to resemble Him? As observed elsewhere, there will be growth, progress, advancement in the life to come. We shall have peace, but it will not be the peace of self-satisfied slumber. We shall have hope, but there will be no restlessness with it. Christ with us will be our hope of glory then, as Christ in us is our hope of glory now.

Col. i. 5. Lastly. How is it that this "hope laid up for us in heaven" is not more of an actual living, consoling, energising force? How little we think of it, speak of it, wish for it, turn it into our consolation and reward!

This world is too much with us, and the world to come too little. Of this let us be assured, and we need neither be surprised at it nor chagrined by it, that He Who is jealous of our love, and craves more of it, and wishes to bestow more of it upon us, and make heaven in our heart long before we join Him there, will sometimes use methods and send messages which have sharpness with them, and rebuke in them. If we set our hearts on the world, He will rob it of so much of its comfort, and honour, and pleasantness, and enjoyment, that the words will force them- *Heb. xiii. 14.* selves out of reluctant but sincere lips, "Here have we no continuing city, but we seek one to come." If our hearts are too much set on the love of children, or the companionship of friends, or the favour of men, or even the discharge of beautiful duty, something happens which brings gall and wormwood into our cup, and saddens us with a sadness that no one can understand but One, Who though in all our afflictions He is afflicted, in the end contrives for us that our sorrow is turned into joy.

When the day comes when there will be no more crying or pain, how much pain and sadness will be over for Him, to whom the ruin of a soul, and the breaking of a life, or the tossing to and fro of a saint writhing in anguish, must mean so much more than they can ever do for us. But this cannot make Him relent from His purpose of deepening our holiness, of knitting us more closely to Himself. So there will be times, often at the close of life, before the last struggle, when hopes seem wrecked, and schemes shattered, and sacrifices unrequited, and seed barren, when the troubled saint turns his face to the wall, and with kindly farewell to friends, and neighbours, who seem quite content to spare him, waits for God and home. "Whom have I in heaven but Thee?" is the question of a heart at last and altogether the Saviour's; in

See cap. vii.

Ps. xxiii 25.

the fulness of the love that reveals itself when we need it, to the voice that whispers, " Surely I come quickly," the reply goes back, " Even so, come, Lord Jesus."

<small>Rev. xxii. 20.</small>

<small>Thomas à Kempis.</small>

" Grant me, most sweet and loving Jesus, to rest in Thee above all things created ; above all health and beauty, above all glory and honour, above all power and dignity, above all knowledge and subtilty, above all riches and arts, above all joy and gladness, above all fame and praise, above all sweetness and consolation, above all hope and promise, above all merit and desire, above all gifts and boons, which Thou canst give and infuse, above all joy and jubilation which the mind can contain and feel : in a word, above all angels and archangels, and all the host of heavens, above all things invisible, and above all that is not Thee, my God."

"The next life seems all so vague to us. We reach out after it. We believe in it, but how hard it is for us to take hold of it! How can we? Only by living here with Him Who is to bring us there—to welcome all His dealings now so cordially, that we shall know our Leader when He opens the last great door—to be always following Him so obediently, that we shall have faith to follow Him even when He leads us into the river and into darkness—this and only this is readiness for death."

BY THE LATE A. W. THOROLD, D.D.,
Lord Bishop of Winchester.

The Tenderness of Christ.
Fourth Thousand. Crown 8vo, 3s. 6d.

Questions of Faith and Duty.
Fourth Thousand. Crown 8vo, 5s.

The Yoke of Christ.
Twelfth Thousand. Crown 8vo, 5s.

The Gospel of Christ.
Sixth Thousand. Crown 8vo, 4s. 6d.

The Presence of Christ.
Twentieth Thousand. Crown 8vo, 3s. 6d.

The Claim of Christ on the Young.
Fourth Thousand. Crown 8vo, 2s. 6d.

On Children.
Fcap. 8vo, cloth, 1s. net.

On the Loss of Friends.
Fcap. 8vo, cloth 1s. net. Paper, sewed, 3d.

On Being Ill.
Fcap. 8vo, cloth, 1s. net. Paper, sewed, 3d.

ISBISTER & CO., LIMITED,
15 & 16 Tavistock St., Covent Garden, W.C.

Printed by BALLANTYNE, HANSON & CO.
London & Edinburgh

www.ingramcontent.com/pod-product-compliance
Lightning Source LLC
Chambersburg PA
CBHW021401230426
43666CB00006B/605